SQE 1 PREP COURSE

CONTRACT LAW

BY ANASTASIA & ANDREW VIALICHKA

First Edition

Published by MetExam
https://metexam.co.uk

(m)etexam

ISBN: 978-1-917053-04-4

ISBN: 978-1-917053-22-8 (Hardcover)

The information provided in this book is subject to change without notice and should not be construed as a commitment by the authors or the publisher. While every effort has been made to ensure the accuracy of the information contained herein, the authors and publisher assume no responsibility for any errors or omissions, or for damages resulting from the use of the information contained in this book.

This publication is designed exclusively for educational purposes, serving as a comprehensive study aid for individuals preparing for the SQE 1 examination. It should not be construed as offering legal advice or as an authoritative resource on legal matters. Its primary objective is to facilitate learning and exam preparation.

Authors: Vialichka, Anastasia; Vialichka, Andrew
Title: Contract Law. SQE 1 Prep Course / Anastasia Vialichka, Andrew Vialichka
Description: First Edition | London: MetExam, 2024
Identifiers: ISBN 978-1-917053-04-4
Subjects: LCSH Contract Law—United Kingdom—Examinations, questions, etc. | Contract Law—England—Examinations, questions, etc. | Contract Law—Wales—Examinations, questions, etc. | Common Law Contracts—United Kingdom—Case Studies. | Legal education in Contract Law—United Kingdom. | Legal education in Contract Law—England. | Legal education in Contract Law—Wales.

INTRODUCTION

INTRODUCTION

Welcome to the foundational stone of your journey towards becoming a solicitor in England and Wales. This text is meticulously crafted as part of a comprehensive MetExam training course designed to prepare you for the Solicitors Qualifying Examination. It lays out the intricate legal tapestry you are about to navigate, providing you with the essential knowledge and analytical tools needed to succeed.

Embrace the learning that awaits, and let this book be your guide and ally on the path to legal proficiency and excellence.

Throughout this text, authors draw upon a wealth of legal scholarship and case law. While specific contributions are not cited in the body of the book, a comprehensive list of all works referenced can be found at the end. These references serves as an acknowledgment of the significant works that have informed this text and as a resource for readers seeking to explore the subject matter further.

CHAPTER 1. AN OVER-VIEW OF CONTRACT FORMATION

1. Defining Contract

The sphere of contract law, a distinct segment of civil law, focuses on the regulations governing individual interactions. This is in stark contrast to criminal law, which oversees societal conduct.

In contract law, remedies primarily aim for compensation, diverging from the punitive measures typical in criminal law. While English law does not provide a strict definition of a contract, it can be conceptualised as an agreement with legal enforceability, imposing obligations on the involved parties. Non-compliance with these obligations allows the aggrieved party to seek a remedy.

Fundamental to contract law is the concurrence of the parties' intentions to establish a legally binding relationship, underpinned by consideration – a mutual exchange of value to validate the agreement.

The simultaneous presence of mutual agreement, intent to create legal relations, and consideration is imperative for the constitution of a legitimate contract.

2. Categories of Contracts

2.1 Forms of Simple Contracts

Simple contracts are characterised by their flexibility in formation, as they can be established in various formats: in writing, verbally, or implied by the actions and behaviour of the parties involved.

2.2 Written Contract Requirements

Specific types of contracts are mandated by law to be documented in writing.

These encompass:

(a) **Guarantee agreements,** where an individual (the guarantor) commits to ensure that another party fulfils their obligations, such as the repayment of a debt;

(b) **Contracts involving the sale, purchase, or alteration** of rights in land or property;

(c)   **Agreements related to consumer credit facilities.**

It is also noteworthy that contracts formed electronically, which are commonplace in consumer dealings, are treated on par with written contracts and are considered legally binding and properly executed.

2.3 Execution of Contracts through Deed

A deed is a special type of document, explicitly identified as a deed, and it needs to be formally executed in the presence of a witness and delivered to be effective.

'Delivery' in this case signifies the manifest intention of the parties to be legally bound by the terms of the deed, often evidenced by wording such as "Delivered as a deed on [date]."

Certain agreements require formation via a deed to attain legal enforceability, including:

(a)   **Unilateral Promises.** Unilateral promises, where no reciprocal benefit or promise is received, can still be legally binding when made through a deed. A common instance is a commitment to give a gift.

(b) **Transfer of Property Rights.** The legal process of transferring property rights, particularly in the context of land, necessitates execution by way of a deed.

Extended Claim Period for Contracts by Deed:

A significant distinction between a simple contract and a contract by deed is the duration within which a breach of contract claim can be initiated.

For non-deed contracts, the limitation period for bringing a claim is six years from the date of the breach. In contrast, for contracts by deed, this period extends to 12 years following the breach.

This extended timeframe is a key reason why some parties opt for contracts by deed even when there are no other compelling reasons for this formality.

CHAPTER 2. AGREEMENT

1. The Nature of an Offer

An offer endows the offeree with the capacity to accept, simultaneously imposing a potential obligation on the offeror. To qualify as an offer, the communication must engender a reasonable belief in the offeree that the offeror is prepared to forge a contract based on the essential terms proposed.

1.1 Expression of Willingness

For a communication to be recognised as an offer, it must manifest a willingness in the form of a promise, undertaking, or commitment to engage in a contract, distinguishing it from a mere invitation to initiate negotiations. It should reflect a clear intent to enter into a contractual agreement. Not every statement in the negotiation phases constitutes an offer.

For instance, if Clara says to David, "I intend to sell my laptop to you for £400," this statement qualifies as a definitive offer.

1.2 Specificity and Exactitude of Terms

The terms of an offer must be articulated with specificity and exactitude. This means that the terms cannot be nebulous or partial.

The essential point is whether the key terms are detailed enough to render a contract enforceable if they were to be included. The particulars of the agreement, especially the subject matter, need to be distinctly specified, as enforceability hinges on a court's ability to determine the specifics of the promise.

For instance, if Emma tells Jack, "I agree to sell you this particular bicycle for £250," it clearly and precisely outlines the intent, identifying both the item and its price. On the other hand, if Emma says to Jack, "I might sell a bicycle for something like £250," it lacks clear commitment, specificity regarding which bicycle is being offered, and a fixed price.

1.3 Offer Notification to the Offeree

For an offeree to possess the capacity to accept, they must be aware of the offer's existence. Consequently, the offer must be effectively communicated to them. An offer can be directed towards a specific individual or group or be made universally, addressing the general public.

1.4 Communications not Constituting an Offer

(a) Responses to Requests for Information. Replying to a request for specific information only sometimes qualifies as an offer.

Consider a situation where a potential buyer emails a car dealer asking, "What is the best price you can offer for the 2020 Model X car?" The dealer responds, "The best price for the 2020 Model X is £15,000."

This response by the dealer does not amount to an offer. It merely provides information in response to the enquiry and does not represent a binding commitment to sell the car at that price.

(b) Invitations to Treat. An invitation to treat is a preliminary step in contractual negotiations, distinct from an actual offer. It typically signifies an invitation for the other party to submit an offer.

In a scenario where Clara asks Emma if she would be interested in buying Clara's bike for £300, Clara's query represents an invitation to treat. Emma can respond with an offer to buy the bike, which may lead to further negotiations or an acceptance.

- **Advertisements as Invitations to Treat.** Typically, advertisements are treated as invitations to treat rather than definitive offers. This approach mitigates the risk of contractual breaches due to the limited availability of products.

For example, if a retailer advertises only five computers in a newspaper, treating the advertisement as an offer could lead to contractual liabilities with every respondent after the fifth, exceeding the available stock.

Therefore, an advertisement invites potential buyers to make their offers, leaving the seller with the discretion to accept or reject them based on availability and other factors.

- **The Nature of Shop Displays.** Products displayed in a shop window or on store shelves constitute invitations to treat, not direct offers to sell. Taking an item to the cashier is the customer's offer to purchase. The transaction is completed, and the offer is accepted when the cashier processes the payment. This system ensures store owners retain control over sales, allowing them to manage situations like stock shortages or incorrect pricing.

- **Retail Display as Invitation to Treat.** Items showcased in retail store windows or on shelves represent invitations to treat, not direct sales offers. The customer's action of taking the goods to the checkout constitutes an offer to buy. This offer is accepted when the retailer processes the sale at the till.

- **Price Lists as Preliminary Engagements.** Price lists are generally regarded in the same vein as advertisements, serving as preliminary engagements rather than firm offers. If a price list were treated as an offer, the issuer would be bound to sell to anyone who accepts by placing an order, potentially exceeding their available stock.

Imagine a car accessories distributor issues a price catalogue for various Volkswagen parts. This catalogue is an invitation to treat, not a concrete offer. Should a garage place an order for Volkswagen brake pads based on this catalogue, their order constitutes an offer. The distributor can accept or decline this offer due to potential difficulties in sourcing sufficient brake pads.

- **Invitations to Tender.** An invitation to tender calls interested entities to present bids detailing their readiness to undertake a specific task. It is not an offer, as agreeing to every tender would result in contractual breaches. The bids tendered are the offers.

A bookstore chain requires an upgraded point-of-sale system. It invites bids from software companies, where they detail the services and terms they can provide. This request is an invitation to treat, not an outright offer. The proposals made by the software companies are the offers, allowing the bookstore chain to select the most suitable one to accept.

- **Auction Procedures as Preliminary Invitations.** In auctions, a catalogue serves not as a definitive offer but as an invitation to treat. This status permits the owner or auctioneer to retract items from the sale before the auction begins. Similarly, when an auctioneer calls for bids, this is an invitation to treat. The auction attendees propose offers through their bids, which they can revoke before the auctioneer finalises the sale with the hammer's fall. The hammer's descent indicates the auctioneer's acceptance of the highest valid bid, assuming it meets any set reserve price.

- **Interpreting Price Quotations.** Classifying a price quotation as either an offer or an invitation to treat depends significantly on the intentions of the involved parties, often discerned from their preceding interactions. In an academic or exam setting, it's less common to be tasked with making intricate judgments regarding the nature of price quotations.

(c) **The Special Case of Unilateral Contracts.** Unilateral contracts represent a unique category where the usual rules are altered. Specifically, advertisements in these instances do constitute offers. A unilateral contract is established when the offeror pledges to perform a particular action if the offeree performs a specified task and the offeree completes that task. These contracts are termed 'unilateral' because only the offeror has an obligation (such as a promise of payment) when making the offer. The offeree can accept and become bound to the contract solely through performance. Often, these offers are made to the public, typically via advertisements, like promising a reward for specific actions. These advertisements are considered offers, as the offeror's intent to be legally bound is evident.

Consider a situation where a fitness company advertises a challenge: "Complete our 30-day fitness program without missing a day and receive £500." The company also announces that it has set aside £20,000 to pay out these rewards, showing its commitment to the offer. A participant enrols in the program and diligently follows the regimen every day, but the company then refuses to pay the £500 upon completion.

In this case, a court will likely determine that the advertisement was an offer for a unilateral contract, which the participant accepted by fully adhering to the program's terms. Completing the challenge, as specified in the advertisement, would constitute a valid acceptance.

2. Discontinuation of an Offer

An offer loses its validity for acceptance once it has been terminated. Termination can arise from actions by either the offeror or the offeree or due to legal stipulations.

2.1 Withdrawal by the Offeror

The offeror has the prerogative to withdraw an offer, a process known as revocation. Revocation involves the offeror retracting their offer.

This can be executed by directly notifying the offeree of the withdrawal before they have accepted the offer.

Alternatively, revocation can occur indirectly if the offeree receives:

- **reliable information,**

- **from a credible source,**

- suggesting that the **offeror has taken actions** which reasonably imply they no longer intend to maintain the offer (such as the offeree learning from a dependable third party that the offeror has sold the car previously offered to a different buyer).

(a) **Conditions for Effective Revocation.** A revocation becomes valid only when the offeree acknowledges it. It is optional for the offeror to personally communicate the revocation; it can be conveyed effectively by a reliable third party, as illustrated earlier.

(b) **Restrictions on Revocation by the Offeror.** While offerors typically have the discretion to withdraw offers any time before they are accepted, there are certain conditions under which this freedom is limited:

- **The Role of Collateral Contracts:** In a collateral contract, the offeree provides something of value (consideration) in return for the offeror's promise, such as the assurance not to revoke a given offer. Further exploration of collateral contracts will occur subsequently.

Imagine a scenario where Charles offers to sell his vintage car to Diana for £50,000 and agrees to keep the offer valid for 60 days if Diana pays £500 as consideration for this extension. Diana pays the £500 as agreed. If Charles decides to revoke his offer after 20 days, he will breach the terms of the collateral contract established by Diana's payment.

- **Commencement of Performance in Unilateral Contracts.** In unilateral contracts, once the offeree begins to perform the task outlined in the offer, the offer becomes irrevocable. It would be inequitable for the offeror to withdraw their offer after the offeree has commenced fulfilling the requested action. However, it's important to note that a binding contract only materialises upon the completion of the performance by the offeree, who retains the right to withdraw at any point until then.

Consider a situation where a mother offers her car to her son, stating that if he completes his university degree, the car will be his. This proposition is an offer in a unilateral contract, with only the mother making a promise. The son has yet to make a formal promise, but he can accept the offer by fulfilling the condition set by his mother. If the son enrols and starts his university education, it would be deemed unfair for the mother to retract her offer.

- **Differentiating the Commencement of Performance in Bilateral Contracts.** Bilateral contracts emerge from offers that a promise or performance can accept. On the other hand, an offer in a unilateral contract is only obtained through performance, as previously discussed. In a bilateral contract, if the offeror has not specified a particular method of acceptance, the commencement of performance by the offeree equates to acceptance. Consequently, this action solidifies the offer, making its revocation infeasible.

It's crucial to note that beginning performance in a bilateral contract mirrors that in a unilateral contract — once performance is initiated, the offer can no longer be terminated. However, the underlying logic differs. In a bilateral contract, starting performance doesn't just render the offer irrevocable but also acts as an acceptance, thus forming a contract.

Consider a scenario where a retailer offers to buy 500 units of a specific product from a supplier at £10 per unit, signalling a bilateral contract since the mode of acceptance isn't restricted to performance. Hence, the supplier can accept either by confirming via email or by starting the process of supplying the 500 units. If the supplier opts to get through the commencement of supply (like packaging the products for delivery), this action constitutes acceptance, and the contract is effectively formed at that point.

2.2 Offer Termination by Offeree

An offeree can bring an offer to an end through rejection, either explicitly or implicitly, as with a counteroffer.

(a) **Direct Rejection.** A direct or express rejection occurs when the offeree explicitly communicates their decision not to accept the offer. Such a rejection effectively terminates the offer, preventing any future acceptance by the offeree should they change their mind. This rejection becomes valid when it reaches the offeror.

Consider a situation where a property developer offers to buy a plot of land for £800,000. The landowner explicitly states the land is worth more, suggesting a value of £850,000 instead. Later, the landowner decides to accept the original £800,000 offer. The initial offer is terminated due to the earlier rejection, meaning no contract exists under the terms.

(b) **The Dynamics of a Counteroffer.** A counter offer arises when the offeree responds to the original offer with a new proposal concerning the same subject but with altered terms (e.g., "I'm interested in purchasing the property at the stated price, provided you include the existing furniture."). A counteroffer serves two functions: it acts as a rejection of the initial offer and establishes a new offer. This process concludes the original offer and changes the roles of the involved parties: the offeree who presents the counteroffer becomes the new offeror, allowing the original offeror to either accept or decline this new proposal.

An artist offers to sell a painting to a collector for £10,000. The collector responds, "I will buy it for £9,000." This response is a counteroffer. It effectively rejects the artist's initial offer of £10,000, and the collector's later attempt to accept the original price would not result in a contract.

The crucial difference now is the collector's counteroffer, which the artist can get. Should the artist agree to this new price of £9,000, a contract to sell the painting at this revised amount would be established.

- **Clarifying Enquiry vs. Counteroffer.** It's important to distinguish between a counteroffer, which effectively rejects the original offer, and a simple enquiry or request for additional information. An enquiry does not end the offer if it implies that the offeree is still considering the original proposal. The deciding factor is whether a reasonable person would interpret the response as rejecting the initial offer.

A property developer offers a plot of land to a prospective buyer for £200,000. The buyer responds by querying if the developer would consider a price reduction of £10,000. This question constitutes a mere enquiry. A reasonable person listening to this exchange would not conclude that the initial offer has been rejected but that the buyer is seeking further information while contemplating the original offer.

(c) **Handling Collateral Contract Rejections.**
When an original offer is accompanied by a collateral contract, which typically involves an agreement to keep the offer open for a fee, a rejection or a counteroffer concerning the collateral contract does not cancel the original offer. The offeree retains the option to accept the primary offer.

Charles offers to sell a vintage car to Diana for £30,000, proposing to keep the offer open for a month if Diana pays £200 for this period. Diana responded that she wouldn't pay £200 but would pay £100 to keep the offer open. By doing so, Diana is rejecting Charles' terms for the collateral contract.

However, Charles' initial offer to sell the car for £30,000 remains valid and open for Diana's acceptance.

(d) **Offer Termination due to Time Elapse.** An offer becomes void if not accepted within the time frame outlined in the offer or if no time limit is specified within a period deemed reasonable. The definition of 'reasonable' is contextual and depends on the nature of the contract's subject matter.

For example, an offer to sell technology products like the latest smartphones might lapse quicker than an offer for more stable commodities like furniture, considering the rapid pace of technological advancements and market trends.

Similarly, offers related to time-sensitive services, such as a limited-time promotional deal for a service, would require prompt acceptance before the promotion ends.

3. Defining Acceptance

In the context of contract formation, acceptance signifies an unequivocal agreement to the stipulated terms of an offer.

This concurrence must be absolute and without deviation, as any alteration or qualification to the terms constitutes a counteroffer. Creating a counteroffer extinguishes the original offer, thus precluding its subsequent acceptance in its original guise.

3.1 Eligibility for Acceptance

The capacity to accept an offer is confined to the individual or entity to whom the offer is specifically addressed. This also extends to group members targeted by the offer, such as an offer made to all subscribers of a specific magazine, where any subscriber can accept the offer.

(a) **Limitations on Transfer of Acceptance Rights.** Generally, the right to accept an offer cannot be transferred to another party. However, it's essential to consider the principles of agency, where an agent can agree to an offer on behalf of their principal. In such cases, the resultant contract is formed between the offeror and the principal, not the agent.

3.2 Awareness of Offer for Acceptance

For an acceptance to be valid, the offeree must be aware of the offer, whether for a standard bilateral or a unilateral contract.

Therefore, in a cross-offer situation, where two parties independently send offers to each other with identical terms, unaware of the other's offer, no contract is formed despite the matching terms.

3.3 Selecting the Mode of Acceptance

In cases where the offeror does not prescribe a specific method, an offer can be accepted in any reasonably suitable manner, given the prevailing conditions.

In bilateral contracts, this acceptance may take the form of a commitment to perform or by beginning the performance itself.

This contrasts unilateral contracts, which necessitate completing the requested action for acceptance.

(a) **Prescribed Acceptance Method by the Offeror.** If the offeror has set out a specific mode of acceptance, and the offeree does not adhere to this prescribed method, the acceptance is typically considered invalid. An exception to this rule is when the offeree's chosen method, though different, is no less favourable to the offeror.

(b) **The Non-Validity of Silence for Acceptance.** Under normal circumstances, an offeree cannot be compelled to respond, nor can their silence be interpreted as accepting an offer. Contractual obligations necessitate affirmative actions from the offeree to indicate their agreement. Silence, inherently, fails to qualify as such an action due to its inherent ambiguity and the uncertainty surrounding the offeree's intentions. While this rule has occasional exceptions, they are exceptional and infrequent.

3.4 Acceptance in Unilateral Contracts

An offer in a unilateral contract is characterised by the offeror seeking an action rather than a promise.

In such cases, the offeror commits to fulfilling their part of the agreement upon the offeree's completion of the specified act. The contract is established once this act is entirely performed.

(a) **No Compulsion for Offeree to Finalise Performance.** In the context of unilateral contracts, it is generally understood that acceptance is only achieved upon the completion of the specified act. Notably, the offeree is not obligated to see the performance through to completion simply because they have initiated it, as only the full completion of the specified act amounts to acceptance of the unilateral offer.

For instance, Maria announces a reward of £300 for anyone who can successfully locate her lost dog. Having some clues about the dog's possible whereabouts, James begins the search. However, he is not legally bound to persist in his search efforts because a contract only comes into existence upon the successful location of the dog.

(b) **Requirement of Notification.** In most cases, the offeree in a unilateral contract is not obligated to inform the offeror when they start the requested performance. However, it is typically necessary for the offeree to notify the offeror within a reasonable timeframe after completing the performance. This requirement ensures that the offeror is aware of the completion of the terms and can fulfil their part of the contract accordingly.

3.5 Communication of Acceptance

Typically, the acceptance of an offer in a bilateral contract must be explicitly communicated to the offeror unless the offer specifically states that no such communication is necessary.

3.6 Conduct as a Form of Acceptance

An offeree's actions can serve as a valid form of acceptance of an offer. It's essential, however, for the offeror to be made aware of the offeree's conduct, meeting the communication requirement for acceptance.

This approach is particularly relevant in business transactions where actions, rather than explicit verbal or written communication, signify acceptance.

A freelance graphic designer offers to create a website for a local café at a quoted price. The café owner responds, suggesting a slightly lower price. The designer starts working on the website without explicitly accepting or rejecting this counteroffer. The commencement of work in this scenario would be interpreted as acceptance of the café owner's counteroffer.

3.7 Effectiveness of Acceptance via Post

The postal rule in contract law dictates that acceptance via post is considered adequate at the time of posting, not when it is received.

This holds true even if the acceptance letter is lost in transit, with a **few exceptions:**

- The letter must **be correctly addressed and appropriately stamped**. If it fails in this regard, the postal rule does not apply.

- The use of postal services to communicate acceptance must **be reasonable**. If it's unreasonable, the rule is not applicable.

- The offer itself may explicitly or implicitly require that acceptance is **only effective upon receipt**. In such cases, parties are regarded as opting out of the postal rule.

It's important to note that the postal rule applies explicitly to accepting offers and does not extend to other contractual communications, such as offer rejections or revocations.

(a) **Application to Immediate Communication Channels.** The postal rule is irrelevant for immediate communication modes such as email. Acceptance through these methods results in the formation of a contract at the point when the offeror actually receives the acceptance. For instance, the contract is formed with email when the offeror reads the acceptance email. This principle aligns with the instantaneous nature of these communication methods, ensuring that the contract is established when both parties are contemporaneously aware of the acceptance.

3.8 Navigating the 'Battle of the Forms'

This term refers to a frequent complication in commercial agreements where each party seeks to contract under their standard terms, which usually differ. The legal challenge is ascertaining whose terms prevail when both sets are referenced during negotiations. The general legal stance is that the contract is formed under the last communicated terms, provided they were not objected to and the contract's execution has begun.

In simpler terms, "the last shot" in this battle of terms, meaning the final set of terms proposed that is followed by contract performance, tends to dictate the contract's conditions.

(a)   **Effectiveness of 'Prevail' Clauses.** Frequently, an offeror incorporates a 'prevail clause' in their proposed contract, asserting that their terms override any others introduced by the offeree. This clause is designed to grant the offeror a strategic advantage in the 'battle of the forms'. However, the practical impact of these clauses is subject to debate. When an offeree counters with their terms, this action is typically viewed as a complete rejection of the original offer, including the 'prevail clause'. As a result, such clauses often fail to enforce the offeror's terms as the dominant ones in the contract.

CHAPTER 3. LEGAL INTENT AND CAPACITY IN CONTRACT FORMATION

1. Presumed Intentions based on Party Relationships

1.1 In Domestic Contexts

In domestic agreements (such as those between spouses or within a family), an underlying assumption exists that the parties do not seek legal enforceability of their arrangements. This assumption, however, can be overturned by objective evidence suggesting otherwise.

Nevertheless, suppose one party knows the other does not intend to create a legally binding agreement. In that case, the arrangement will not hold legal weight despite any objective indications of such intent.

Imagine two siblings agreeing to contribute equally to renovating their inherited family home. Under normal circumstances, this agreement wouldn't be considered legally binding.

However, if they make this agreement while formalising the division of their late parent's estate, which includes the family home, this context could provide substantial objective evidence indicating their intention to create a legally enforceable contract.

1.2 Legal Aspects of Social Arrangements

Social arrangements generally carry a similar presumption against the intention for legal binding. The courts typically assume that there is only intention to create legal obligations if counter-evidence is presented.

Notably, this presumption is often overturned in scenarios where friends or relatives collectively participate in a competitive event or contest, even though the basis of their relationship is primarily social.

Imagine a group of friends who agree to purchase a lottery ticket together, each contributing an equal amount towards the purchase. They make a verbal agreement to share any winnings equally. If their ticket wins a significant prize, the law will enforce the agreement, requiring the winnings to be transferred as per their initial agreement.

This situation deviates from a typical social arrangement as it forms an informal consortium, indicating an intention to create legal relations beyond mere social interaction.

1.3 Assessing Intent in Commercial Engagements

There's a robust assumption in commercial interactions that the parties aim to establish a legally binding contract. Overturning this presumption requires unequivocal evidence, with courts adopting an objective perspective in evaluating such evidence.

Due to this strong presumption and the frequent practice of formalising commercial agreements in writing, instances where attempts are made to challenge this assumption are rare.

(a)   **Overcoming the Presumption.** To challenge the presumption of legal intent in commercial agreements, parties might specify that the agreement is 'binding in honour only' or 'subject to contract'. These phrases indicate ongoing negotiations and a current lack of intent to be legally bound. In the context of 'subject to contract', it is implied that a legally binding contract will ensue later. A statement made spontaneously or in a state of anger might also suffice to negate the presumption of legal intent.

(b) **Distinguishing Between Social and Commercial Interactions.** Determining whether a discussion is social or commercial can be challenging. In such cases, courts will consider the entirety of the circumstances to ascertain whether the parties intended to establish a binding contract.

Imagine a scenario where Raj, the owner of a small tech startup, verbally agrees with Priya, a freelance developer, to pay her a bonus of £20,000 if her software development significantly increases the company's revenue. This conversation happens during a casual coffee meeting without formal agreement or written documentation.

Despite critical elements of a contract, the setting and the informal nature of the discussion, combined with the lack of proper acknowledgement or subsequent follow-up, suggest that there was no genuine intention to create a legally binding contract.

In this case, the agreement appears more akin to an informal, aspirational promise rather than a concrete commercial commitment.

2. Legal Capacity for Contractual Agreement

A party must possess the intent to form a legal contract and the legal capacity to enter into one. The law offers protection to specific vulnerable groups, such as minors and individuals with mental incapacities, shielding them from the obligations of contracts they might not fully understand or intend to engage in. A contract becomes unenforceable if one party lacks the necessary capacity.

2.1 Legal Position of Minors (Individuals Under 18 Years)

As a general principle, contracts involving minors are voidable at the minor's discretion. While minors have the right to enforce contracts, they are not legally obligated to honour them unless they confirm ('ratify') the contract after age 18.

(a) Notable Exceptions:

- **'Necessaries':** Contracts made by minors for vital goods or services, provided the cost is reasonable, are enforceable. The Sale of Goods Act 1979 defines 'necessaries' as goods appropriate to the minor's social and economic status and their actual requirements during the transaction. What constitutes a necessity is subjective and varies for each individual.

- **Employment Contracts:** Minors can validly enter into employment contracts, assuming the terms are advantageous.

- **Property Acquisition Contracts:** Minors are also bound by contracts for acquiring a long-term interest in property (such as shares in a company) unless they explicitly renounce the contract. This binding nature arises from the minor's acquisition of real ownership rights under the contract.

(b) **The Minors' Contracts Act 1987.** The general rule exempting minors from their contractual obligations can sometimes be unjust to the other contracting party. For instance, a minor may receive a car from a seller but refuse to pay. The Minors Contracts Act 1987 allows courts to intervene to address such imbalances. Under this Act, if a minor has received property from another party, the court can order the minor to return the property if deemed fair and appropriate.

2.2 Understanding Contracts with Mental Capacity Considerations

When an individual lacking mental capacity enters into a contract, such a contract is revocable by that individual, provided the other contracting party is aware of their mental incapacity.

As outlined in the Mental Capacity Act 2005 (MCA), a person is deemed to lack the mental capacity for contracting if they cannot understand, retain, evaluate, or communicate the information relevant to the decision.

(a) **Ratification After Regaining Capacity.** Should an individual who lacked mental capacity at the time of a contract's inception later regain this capacity, they are then allowed to ratify the contract, thereby making it valid.

(b) **Responsibility for Essential Goods and Services.** In alignment with the MCA, individuals who lack mental capacity are still expected to pay a reasonable price for essential goods or services ('necessaries'). This provision mirrors the legal treatment of minors, ensuring a level of responsibility for necessary transactions despite the lack of total mental capacity.

2.3 Contractual Validity in Cases of Intoxication

In instances where an individual is so significantly intoxicated that they lose the capacity to understand their actions, paralleling mental incapacity, the legal treatment of their contracts is nuanced. These individuals must pay a reasonable amount for necessary items or services.

However, they are not legally bound to fulfil other contractual obligations if the other party is conscious of their intoxicated condition. Although there is no direct legal precedent concerning the influence of drugs or other similar substances, it's generally inferred that the legal stance would align with that of alcohol-induced intoxication.

2.4 Contractual Authority of Incorporated Companies

As a distinct legal personality, an incorporated company possesses its contractual capacity separate from its shareholders.

According to the Companies Act 2006, the legitimacy of a company's actions cannot be questioned on the grounds of lacking capacity, disregarding any contrary stipulations in the company's constitution.

This provision reinforces that incorporated companies have an inherent legal authority to engage in contractual agreements autonomously.

CHAPTER 4. THE PRIN-CIPLE OF CONSIDERA-TION

In contract law, a court will only recognise an agreement as a contract if there is consideration from both parties or an accepted substitute for consideration. Consideration is "an act, forbearance, or the promise thereof by one party".

Typically, this involves one party paying or promising to pay money in return for the other party's performance of a task or delivery of an item or the promise thereof. A common form of consideration is an agreement not to sue, a forbearance from acting.

In essence, consideration is the value exchanged for the promise or action of the other party. It can manifest as either a positive action or a refraining from action (negative obligation).

1. Distinction between Executed and Executory Consideration

In contract law, the nature of consideration is classified as executed or executory. Executory consideration refers to a promise of an act or forbearance in the future. When this act or forbearance is performed, the consideration becomes executed.

Particularly in unilateral contracts—where the offeror promises a reward upon the offeree's completion of a specific task, like finding a lost item—the performance of the task can simultaneously serve as the acceptance of the offer and the performance of consideration.

A homeowner, Lisa, promises to pay £500 to a gardener, John if he can landscape her garden within two weeks. John agrees and starts the work.

Until John finishes the landscaping, the consideration remains executive on both sides: John's performance of the landscaping service and Lisa's promise to pay upon completion. Once John completes the landscaping within the agreed time, the consideration becomes executed – John has performed his part of the deal, and Lisa is now bound to pay the £500.

2. The Necessity of Consider- ation from Promisee

In contract law, a crucial tenet is that consideration, the value exchanged in a contract, must originate from the promisee — the individual to whom the promise is made. This means the party seeking to enforce the contract must be the one who has provided the consideration. A notable exception exists for contracts executed as deeds, where consideration is not a prerequisite for enforceability.

The Contracts (Rights of Third Parties) Act 1999 modifies this rule by allowing third parties to enforce specific contract terms. For a third party to exercise this right, they must be named explicitly in the contract, and the contract term they seek to enforce should be intended for their benefit.

For example, Ellen agrees to purchase a car from a dealer for £10,000. Without Ellen's request, Ellen's mother offers to pay the dealer £5,000 towards the car's price.

Despite her mother's payment, the consideration must come from Ellen, the promisee, to form a valid contract between Ellen and the car dealer. The dealer cannot enforce the contract against Ellen's mother, as she is not the promisee in the agreement. Ellen remains responsible for providing the £10,000 consideration as agreed in the contract.

This scenario underscores the principle that the promisee must be the source of consideration in a contract.

3. Legal Sufficiency versus Adequacy of Consideration

In contract law, for consideration to be legally valid, it must possess some degree of value, however minimal. The essence of consideration is to confirm that the contracting parties have mutually agreed to exchange promises or values. The legal system does not delve into assessing the fairness or equity of the deal — it does not judge whether the consideration is adequate or of comparable value to what is being provided by the other party.

However, it's important to note that a significant disparity in the value of consideration may indicate the presence of a vitiating factor. Such a factor could make the contract void or voidable due to elements like mistake or duress.

For instance, if Alice agrees to sell her vintage car, valued at £20,000, to Bob for a nominal sum of £100, the law regards the £100 as sufficient consideration despite its inadequacy compared to the car's value. The courts will not invalidate the contract based on this disparity in value alone.

However, if Alice was coerced into agreeing to this price under duress, or if there was a mistake about the car's value, this inadequacy might be considered evidence of a vitiating factor affecting the contract's validity.

3.1 The Concept of Illusory Consideration

In contract law, while there is considerable leeway in determining the sufficiency of consideration, the courts maintain that consideration must possess genuine legal value and not be entirely imaginary.

This means the consideration must be concrete and not based on an ambiguous or unfulfillable promise. The legal system refrains from intervening in 'bad bargains' or unequal exchanges, focusing instead on ensuring that the consideration is real and has some legal standing, however minimal it may be. The essence here is to differentiate between actual, enforceable promises and vague or purely speculative promises.

Imagine a scenario where Rachel agrees to sell her bicycle to Joey for £50. In return, Joey promises to pay the £50 "if and when he feels like it." In this case, Joey's promise is considered illusory.

The phrase "if and when he feels like it" is too vague and subjective, giving Joey complete discretion over whether or not to pay. This lack of a definitive commitment means that Rachel receives no concrete, enforceable promise in exchange for the bicycle.

Therefore, the contract lacks valid consideration because Joey's promise is not binding or legally enforceable, rendering it illusory.

4. Consideration and the Performance of an Existing Duty

4.1 Fulfilling an Existing Contractual Obligation to the Promisor

In contract law, fulfilling an obligation that one already owes under a contract to the person making a new promise (the promisor) typically does not constitute valid consideration. The action or performance is already a duty bound by the existing contract.

However, if the promise is in exchange for actions that exceed the scope of the initial obligation, then this arrangement can be viewed as forming a new contract. Here, the additional work is the consideration for the other compensation or benefit offered by the promisor.

This principle distinguishes between merely fulfilling an existing duty, which does not provide new consideration, and undertaking extra duties or actions, which can form the basis of a new contractual agreement.

Suppose a construction company, BuildCo, has a contract with a client, Alex, to construct a building for £500,000. Midway through the project, Alex requests an additional feature that was not included in the original contract — a rooftop garden. BuildCo agrees to this other feature and asks for an extra £50,000, to which Alex agrees.

In this scenario, BuildCo's original agreement to construct the building is not a valid consideration for the extra £50,000, as they are already contractually obligated to build it. However, agreeing to add the rooftop garden, which was not part of the original contract, constitutes a new consideration.

This further consideration (the rooftop garden) justifies the additional payment of £50,000 from Alex, effectively creating a new contractual agreement for the extra work.

(a) **The Practical Benefit Exception.** A notable exception concerns the practical benefits of performing an existing contractual duty. When the performance of a current duty provides a tangible, valuable benefit to the party offering additional consideration, this can be deemed a reasonable consideration. For instance, in a construction contract, if completing the work ahead of schedule helps the contractor avoid a penalty for late completion, this accelerated completion may constitute a practical benefit to the client.

However, it's crucial to differentiate between a genuine practical benefit and a situation where the additional consideration is extracted under pressure or duress. If the latter is the case, further consideration may not be recognised as valid since duress undermines the voluntariness of the agreement, an essential aspect of proper contractual consideration.

Consider a scenario where a contractor, Sarah, is building a hotel for a client, David. The contract includes a penalty clause stating that Sarah will incur a significant financial penalty if the construction is not completed by a specific date. As the deadline approaches, unforeseen circumstances delay the project. Sarah informs David that she can still meet the deadline, but only if additional workers are hired, which would increase the cost. David agrees to pay an extra £20,000 to cover these costs.

In this situation, Sarah's original contract obligates her to complete the construction by the deadline. Completing the work she has already been contracted for would be a familiar consideration.

However, her offer to meet the original deadline under the new, more challenging circumstances presents a practical benefit to David — it saves him from the disruptions and potential financial losses of a delayed hotel opening.

David's agreement to pay extra in this context is a valid consideration, as it's for a practical benefit (avoidance of the penalty and timely completion of the hotel) that goes beyond Sarah's initial contractual duty.

4.2 Consideration Involving Performance of a Duty Owed to a Third Party

In contract law, there is a contrasting principle when performing duties owed to a third party. Suppose a party promises to perform or act on an existing contractual duty owed to a third party.

In that case, this can serve as sufficient consideration for a new promise made by the promisor (the person making the new promise). This scenario differs from fulfilling a duty owed directly to the promisor, as it involves obligations to an external party, which can be leveraged as a valid consideration in a separate agreement with the promisor.

This principle recognises that fulfilling an obligation to a third party can create value or benefit in a different contractual relationship and, hence, can constitute valid consideration for a new promise or agreement.

Imagine a scenario where an electrician, Emily, has a contract with a school to perform maintenance work. Separately, Emily enters into a discussion with a construction company, BuildCo, which is renovating a nearby library. BuildCo is running behind schedule and needs additional electrical work done quickly. They approach Emily, and she agrees to prioritise and complete the electrical work at the library, which is outside her existing contract with the school.

In exchange for Emily's commitment to prioritise the library project, BuildCo agrees to pay her an additional fee. Here, Emily's promise to perform her existing duty (electrical work) owed to a third party (the school) is considered sufficient consideration for the new promise from BuildCo (the additional payment).

Even though Emily is already contractually obligated to perform electrical work, her commitment to prioritise the library for BuildCo, affecting her arrangement with the school, creates a new value and forms the basis for a valid contractual agreement with BuildCo.

4.3 Consideration and Statutory Duties

In contractual agreements, fulfilling a duty imposed by statute does not qualify as a valid consideration. This is because statutory duties are obligations that one is already legally required to perform, and thus, offering to perform such duties cannot be considered a new or additional exchange of value in the context of a contract.

For instance, consider a situation where a public house owner offers to pay a police officer £50 per night to maintain law and order around the premises while the officer is on duty. Since preserving law and order is already a statutory duty of the police, this does not constitute valid consideration for the public house owner's promise to pay. The officer is merely performing their existing legal obligation.

However, there are instances where services provided by statutory bodies, such as the police, go beyond their ordinary duties. In such cases, they can legitimately charge for these additional services. Examples include providing extra policing at football matches or during a strike, where the requirements exceed the routine duties of maintaining public order.

5. Prior Acts and Promises

In contract law, acts or promises that occurred before the formation of a contract are not considered valid considerations. Consideration must be contemporary with the contract; it should be a part of the mutual exchange that forms the basis of the contract. Suppose an action or promise was made before the contract was agreed upon.

In that case, it cannot be used as a basis for enforcing the contractual obligations, as it does not represent a present value exchange between the parties.

5.1 The Exception of Implied Understanding for Past Consideration

While past consideration typically does not suffice in contract law, there is an exception when there's an implied understanding of future payment for an act or promise made at the promisor's request.

In such cases, the subsequent promise to pay is viewed not as a new obligation but as determining the amount for the service or action already performed. This understanding retroactively validates the past consideration, making the promise to pay enforceable.

For this exception to apply, three critical conditions must be met:

(a) **Act Performed at Promisor's Request:** The initial action or service must have been undertaken following a request from the promisor.

(b) **Mutual Understanding of Remuneration:** Both parties must have understood when the act was performed that it would be compensated through payment or some other form of benefit.

(c) **Enforceability of the Expected Compensation:** The agreed-upon payment or benefit, if it had been promised before the act was performed, should have been something that could be legally enforced.

This exception acknowledges situations where both parties implied and understood the promise of payment or benefit, even if it's not formalised until after the act has been completed.

6. The Principle of Partial Debt Settlement

Under English law, an agreement to accept a partial payment as a complete debt settlement is typically not legally binding.

For instance, if Alfred owes Beatrice £500 and offers £450 as a full settlement, which Beatrice accepts, she is still legally entitled to claim the remaining £50. This is because Alfred's partial payment does not constitute fresh consideration under the law, which is necessary to enforce Beatrice's promise of accepting a reduced amount.

For such an agreement to be legally binding, Beatrice would need to receive an additional benefit or consideration apart from the reduced payment.

6.1 Recognised Exceptions

There are, however, certain exceptions to this general rule where part payment can be considered sufficient:

(a) **Disputed Debt Settlements:** If the debt amount is under bona fide dispute, an agreement to accept a lesser amount can be valid. Here, the consideration is the settlement of an uncertain debt value.

(b) **Unliquidated Claims:** This applies when the precise amount of debt needs to be fixed or clarified.

(c) **Altered Payment Terms:** This includes scenarios where the creditor gains an advantage, such as receiving a smaller amount earlier than due or at a different location from the one initially agreed upon.

(d) **Third-Party Payments:** If a third party settles a debt under an agreement that the payment will fully discharge the original debtor, the creditor cannot then claim the balance from the original debtor.

(e) **Varied Forms of Payment:** If the creditor agrees to accept a different form of payment (like goods or services) at their request, this can constitute a valid consideration.

(f) **Agreements with Creditors:** A composition agreement is when a debtor negotiates with all their creditors to pay a mutually agreed amount in complete satisfaction of all outstanding debts, usually when facing financial hardship.

These exceptions allow for flexibility and practicality in debt settlements, acknowledging circumstances where the strict application of the part payment rule may not be just or equitable.

7. The Doctrine of Promissory Estoppel

Promissory estoppel is a principle in equity that gives legal force to promises unsupported by consideration. It prevents a party from reneging on their promise under specific conditions based on the notion that they are 'estopped' (legally barred) from doing so.

Importantly, promissory estoppel is a defensive legal tool; it can be used to defend against a claim but cannot be the primary basis for initiating one.

For promissory estoppel to be applicable, **several criteria** must be met:

(a) **Clear Promise:** There must be a distinct and unambiguous promise (whether stated outright or implied) by the promisor to set aside their existing legal rights. An example of this might be agreeing to accept a reduced payment than what was stipulated in the original contract.

(b) **Altered Position Based on Promise:** The promisee must have reasonably relied on the promise and changed their position or acted in a way they wouldn't have had the promise been made.

(c) **Inequity in Revoking the Promise:** It should be demonstrably unfair or unjust for the promisor to retract their promise under the circumstances.

It's important to note that in situations involving ongoing obligations (like rent payments), the effect of promissory estoppel is merely suspensive.

This means that the original rights or obligations are reinstated once the specific circumstances that led to the estoppel cease to exist or after a reasonable notification period. Promissory estoppel, thus, temporarily modifies the terms of the original agreement but doesn't permanently alter them.

CHAPTER 5. THE DOCTRINE OF PRIVITY OF CONTRACT

The doctrine of privity of contract is a fundamental principle in contract law which stipulates that only the parties directly involved in a contract have the legal right to enforce or challenge it. Under this doctrine, a third party not a party to the contract cannot gain rights or be subject to obligations arising from that contract.

Essentially, the rights and duties established by a contract are confined exclusively to the signatories — the individuals or entities that have entered into the contractual agreement.

This principle upholds the notion that a contract cannot confer rights or impose obligations on anyone outside of those who have mutually consented to the terms of the agreement.

Imagine a scenario where a homeowner, Alice, enters into a contract with a builder, Bob, to renovate her house. According to their agreement, Bob will complete the renovation for a specified price. Alice's neighbour, Charlie, prefers a different style of renovation and believes the work will negatively impact the value of his property.

Despite Charlie's concerns, he cannot legally challenge the contract between Alice and Bob or demand changes to the renovation plans. This is because Charlie is not a party to the contract; he is a third party. The rights and obligations of the contract exist solely between Alice and Bob. Not being privy to their agreement, Charlie has no standing to enforce or contest the terms of their contract.

This example demonstrates the core principle of the doctrine of privity of contract, which restricts the enforcement of contractual rights and obligations to the parties who have entered into the contract.

1. Legal Exceptions under Statute

1.1 The Contracts (Rights of Third Parties) Act 1999 and its Impact on Privity

The Contracts (Rights of Third Parties) Act 1999 (CRTPA) significantly modifies English law's traditional doctrine of privity of contract. This Act was introduced to address limitations of the privity doctrine, supplementing various standard law exceptions that had evolved.

The CRTPA provides that a third party — someone not a direct party to the contract — can enforce a term of the contract under certain conditions:

(a) **Express Provision for Third Party Enforcement:** If the contract explicitly states that a third party may enforce a specific term.

(b) **Terms Benefiting a Third Party:** If a contract term is intended to confer a benefit on a third party, and it is clear from the contract that the parties intended this term to be enforceable by the third party.

For a third party to be eligible under the CRTPA, they must be explicitly named or identifiable as a class member intended to benefit from the contract. Interestingly, the third party need not have been in existence when the contract was made. The CRTPA is particularly useful when the contract is intended to benefit someone not directly involved in the agreement.

However, it's important to note that the CRTPA does not allow third parties to be subjected to contractual obligations; it only enables them to benefit from a contract. This distinction maintains the foundational aspect of privity in that obligations under a contract are still confined to the parties involved.

Imagine a couple, John and Emily, planning their wedding and hiring a photographer, Sarah. Their contract with Sarah includes a clause stating that their parents, who are financing the wedding, are entitled to receive a set of the wedding photos.

Although John and Emily's parents are not parties to the contract between John, Emily, and Sarah, the CRTPA allows them to enforce this specific contract term. This is because the contract expressly provides that the parents (third parties in this case) may implement the term regarding receiving wedding photos.

In this scenario, if Sarah fails to provide the photos to the parents as stipulated in the contract, the parents have a legal right under the CRTPA to enforce this contract term despite not being direct parties to it.

This example demonstrates how the CRTPA can be used to confer enforceable rights on third parties who are intended to benefit from a contract.

1.2 Limitations of the Contracts (Rights of Third Parties) Act 1999 (CRTPA)

The CRTPA, while transformative, does not encompass all contractual relationships.

Notably, it does not apply to certain types of contracts, including:

(a) **Employment Contracts:** Agreements between employees and employers.

(b) **Articles of Association:** These documents serve as the internal constitution of a company, detailing the relationship between the company and its share-holders.

Additionally, the CRTPA's applicability is contingent upon the terms of the contract itself. If a contract explicitly states that the CRTPA does not apply, then the rights provided by the Act are not extended to third parties. In practice, many commercial contracts are drafted explicitly with clauses excluding the application of the CRTPA to avoid unintended third-party rights.

1.3 Modifying Contracts with Third-Party Rights Under CRTPA

Under the Contracts (Rights of Third Parties) Act 1999 (CRTPA), specific restrictions exist on altering or nullifying a contract when it involves third-party rights. Suppose a third party has enforceable rights under a contract.

In that case, the primary contracting parties cannot change or terminate the contract to the detriment of the third party unless specific criteria are satisfied. These restrictions are in place to prevent undermining the third party's legally recognised interests.

Specifically, the contract cannot be modified in a way that adversely affects the third party if:

(a) **Consent from the Third Party:** The third party must have explicitly agreed to the term that confers a benefit upon them. This agreement needs to be communicated to the contracting parties.

(b) **Third Party's Reliance on the Term:** The contract term must remain the same if the third party has already relied on it, especially if the promisor is aware of this reliance. This ensures that the third party's actions based on the contract are respected.

(c) **Foreseeable Reliance by the Third Party:** If it is reasonable to expect that the third party would rely on a particular term of the contract and acted based on this expectation, the term cannot be altered without considering the impact on the third party.

These conditions are designed to safeguard the interests and rights of third parties recognised under a contract. They ensure that once a third party's rights are established, they are not arbitrarily revoked or diminished by the actions of the original parties to the contract.

Suppose a software company, TechCorp, enters into a contract with a graphic design firm, DesignCo, to develop a new website. The contract includes a clause stating that a particular freelance photographer, Maria, will receive a credit and a specified payment for her photos used on the website. Although not a party to the contract between TechCorp and DesignCo, Maria is a third party with rights under the contract.

A few months into the project, TechCorp and DesignCo decided to change the website's design and use different photos, which would nullify Maria's credit and payment. However, Maria has already turned down other projects that rely on this contract.

In this scenario, TechCorp and DesignCo cannot simply rescind or alter the contract to remove Maria's credit and payment without her consent due to the following reasons:

Maria's Consent: As the third party who has agreed to the terms benefiting her, her consent is required for any changes affecting her rights.

Maria's Reliance: She has relied on the contract's terms by preceding other opportunities, and TechCorp and DesignCo are aware of this reliance.

Reasonable Expectation of Reliance: It was foreseeable that Maria would rely on the contract terms and act based on this expectation.

Therefore, under the principles of the CRTPA, Maria's rights and expectations must be respected, preventing TechCorp and DesignCo from unilaterally altering the contract to her detriment without her agreement.

2. Refinements to the Privity Doctrine in Common Law

2.1 Agency and Its Relationship to Privity

In the context of agency, a principal delegates an agent to form contracts with third parties on their behalf. Typically, the contract is formed directly between the principal and the third party, making the agent merely an intermediary without party status. This aligns with the privity rule, as the principal is a contractual party.

However, an exception emerges when an agent represents an undisclosed principal, meaning the third party is unaware of the principal's existence. In these scenarios, the agent (provided they have the necessary authority) and the undisclosed principal can enforce or be bound by the contract. This creates a unique exception to the traditional privity rule.

Suppose a businessperson, Mr. Smith, appoints Ms. Johnson as his agent to purchase artwork on his behalf without disclosing his identity.

Ms. Johnson buys a painting under her name from an artist, Mr. Lee. In this situation, Mr. Smith (the undisclosed principal) and Ms. Johnson (the agent) have the right to enforce or be subject to the contract terms with Mr. Lee.

2.2 Assignment of Contractual Rights

Assignment involves transferring the rights of a contract to a third party who was not initially involved in the contract. For an assignment to be valid, the obligated party in the original contract must be notified of this transfer. Only a contract's benefits, not the burdens, can be assigned.

A novation agreement is made if there's a need to transfer the obligations and benefits. In novation, original parties are replaced with new ones, creating a further contractual relationship and circumventing the privity rule.

Laura has a contract with a gym, entitling her to a year's membership. Midway through the year, she assigns her membership benefits to her friend, Mark. She notifies the gym of this assignment. Mark can now use the gym services, but Laura remains liable for the membership fees unless a novation agreement is executed, substituting Mark as the party responsible for the contract.

2.3 The Legal Doctrine of Subrogation

Subrogation is a critical concept in insurance law and the dynamics of guarantor-guarantee relationships. Within the scope of an insurance contract, when an insurer compensates the policyholder for a claim, the insurer is conferred with the policyholder's rights through 'subrogation.'

This legal mechanism allows the insurer to 'step into the shoes' of the policyholder, inheriting the right to pursue any claim the policyholder has against a third party responsible for the loss. Similarly, in the context of guarantor-guarantee relationships, should a guarantor fulfil a financial obligation on behalf of a debtor to a creditor, subrogation grants the guarantor the creditor's rights.

Consequently, the guarantor can pursue the debtor for reimbursement, effectively standing in the creditor's legal position.

Consider a scenario where an insured homeowner, Oliver, suffers property damage due to negligence by a construction firm. If Oliver's insurance company covers the damage costs, subrogation allows the insurer to seek compensation from the construction firm for the damages paid to Oliver.

2.4 The Concept of Collateral Contracts

Collateral contracts are another exception to the principle of privity in contract law. This exception arises when the courts recognise the existence of a collateral contract between the promisor and a third party, existing parallel to the main contract.

Historically, many instances where collateral contracts were identified are now addressed under the Contracts (Rights of Third Parties) Act 1999 (CRTPA), particularly in scenarios where the contract is intended to confer a benefit on a non-party. However, certain situations remain where the CRTPA may not apply, and the concept of a collateral contract becomes pertinent.

A collateral contract is a secondary agreement that complements or adds to the primary contract. It involves separate and distinct promises made between one of the parties to the main contract and a third party. Such contracts offer a way to circumvent the restrictions of privity, allowing third parties some rights or benefits in connection with the central contractual arrangement.

Suppose a car manufacturer advertises that anyone who buys their car from any dealership will receive a free satellite navigation system. A buyer, Jane, purchases the car based on this advertisement but does not receive the navigation system.

Here, Jane could argue the existence of a collateral contract between herself and the manufacturer, based on the advertisement, which runs alongside her purchase contract with the dealership.

This collateral contract, separate from her purchase agreement with the dealer, could provide her with legal grounds to claim the promised navigation system.

2.5 Utilisation of Trusts to Circumvent Privity Issues

Trusts can be employed as a judicial mechanism to navigate around the limitations imposed by the doctrine of privity. When one party, A, promises benefits to another party, B, intended for a third party, C, the courts may determine that B is holding A's promise in trust for C. This arrangement enables C to enforce A's promise, bypassing the typical privity constraints.

Identifying a trust arrangement is most straightforward when the terms 'trust' or 'trustee' are explicitly used in the contractual agreement. However, a trust relationship can be implied based on the contract's content and context even without these terms. The critical factor is the discernible, irrevocable intention to benefit the third party. The courts are generally reluctant to infer a trust if there's no clear indication that creating such a benefit for the third party was the contracting parties' intention.

Consider a scenario where a homeowner, Mr. Green, contracts with a builder, Mr. Brown, to renovate his house. In their agreement, Mr. Green stipulates that a particular payment sum should be explicitly used to hire Mr. Black, a subcontractor, for the electrical work.

If the terms suggest that Mr Brown is to act as a trustee of Mr Green's promise to pay Mr Black for his services, Mr Black might be deemed a beneficiary of this trust. As such, Mr Black could enforce the payment directly against Mr Green, irrespective of the direct contractual relationship between Mr Green and Mr Brown.

This trust mechanism allows Mr. Black, the third party, to enforce his right to payment, circumventing the privity rule.

CHAPTER 6. OUTLINING THE TERMS OF A CONTRACT

Establishing the terms of a contract is a crucial process following the confirmation of the contract's existence. These terms constitute the parties' specific agreements and clauses mutually agreed upon. It's essential to differentiate between these contractual terms and 'representations', preliminary statements made during negotiations but do not form an integral part of the contract, as they entail different legal treatments and remedies.

The terms are usually explicit and delineated in the document for written contracts. In contrast, identifying the exact terms of oral contracts can be more intricate, often requiring examining additional evidence or context to ascertain the agreed-upon stipulations. Even in written contracts, oral statements may supplement the written terms.

However, substantiating these oral statements as part of the contract can be complex due to the parol evidence rule, which restricts the use of external evidence to modify or supplement the written contract. When ambiguous or unclear, interpretation or clarification of terms may be necessary in oral and written contracts.

1. Categories of Contract Terms

Contract terms are typically categorised as either conditions or warranties. They encompass terms explicitly agreed upon by the parties (known as express terms) and those introduced by legal statutes, court decisions, or customary practices (implied terms).

Express terms are those explicitly stated and agreed upon, while implied terms, though not specifically mentioned, are considered an understood part of the contract. Oral contracts often incorporate terms, a concept also relevant in written contracts.

2. Comparing Terms with Representations

Statements made during contract negotiations can become integral parts of the contract (as terms) or remain as external elements (as representations).

This classification hinges on the parties' intent: if a statement is meant to be a binding part of the contract, it becomes a term; if it primarily encourages the other party to enter the contract, it is a representation.

This differentiation is crucial, as it influences the legal recourse and remedies available for breach or misrepresentation.

2.1 Assessing if a Statement is a Term or Representation

Classifying a statement as a term or a representation in a contract hinges on the parties' intentions, as assessed objectively. This assessment is based on how a reasonable person, considering the conduct and interactions of the parties, would interpret the statement.

When a contract is documented in writing, the omission of a specific oral statement often leads courts to infer that the statement was intended as a representation rather than a contractual term.

Several key factors are considered in this determination:

(a) **Relative Importance of the Statement:** The significance of the statement to the party it was made to is a critical factor. Suppose the statement was pivotal to the decision to enter into the contract, suggesting the party would not have agreed to the contract without it. In that case, it is more likely to be regarded as a contractual term.

(b) **Timing of the Statement:** The point during the negotiations when the statement was made also influences its classification. Statements made when the contract is formed are more likely to be terms, whereas those made during initial discussions are typically viewed as representations.

(c) **Expertise or Special Knowledge:** The nature of the party making the statement is also relevant. Suppose the party has specialist knowledge or skills and makes a factual statement within the scope of their expertise, intending for the other party to rely on it. The statement will likely be construed as a contract term in that case. Conversely, if the statement expresses belief or opinion without direct knowledge, it is classified as a representation.

These factors help discern whether a statement is an integral part of the contract or a persuasive element used during the negotiation phase.

Significance of Differentiating Between Terms and Representations:

Understanding whether a statement in a contract negotiation is a term or a representation is crucial due to the different legal remedies available if the statement proves false. If a statement is a contractual term, any non-compliance constitutes a breach of contract, entitling the innocent party to claim damages.

In contrast, if the statement is a misrepresentation (not incorporated into the contract), the nature of the remedy depends on whether the misrepresentation was innocent, negligent, or fraudulent. While damages may still be recoverable for misrepresentation, they are typically less substantial than those awarded for a breach of contract.

This distinction underscores the importance of accurately identifying the nature of statements in contract law.

3. Categorising Contract Terms: Conditions and Warranties

Whether express or implied, contract terms are classified as conditions or warranties. This classification impacts the available remedies in the event of a breach. A breach of a condition allows the innocent party to terminate the contract, whereas a breach of a warranty does not. If it needs to be clarified whether a term is a condition or a warranty, it falls into a third category known as 'innominate terms'.

It's important to note that the classification of a term as a condition or warranty is not solely determined by its label in the contract. The courts examine the term's actual impact on the contract's operation, and a term labelled as a condition might not necessarily allow contract termination if the breach is trivial.

3.1 Conditions in Contracts

A condition in a contract is a fundamental term that is central to the contract's functionality. Breaching a condition means the contract cannot effectively operate without it. Such a breach, often termed a 'repudiatory breach', indicates that the breaching party is effectively rejecting the contract. Consequently, the innocent party can terminate the contract and seek damages.

However, if the innocent party opts to continue with the contract (known as 'affirming' it), they forfeit the right to terminate but retain the right to claim damages.

3.2 The Role of Warranties in Contractual Agreements

In contrast to conditions, a warranty is a term in a contract that is considered incidental or supplementary to the primary stipulations of the agreement. Warranties do not form the core of the contract, and as such, breaches of warranties are viewed as less severe by the courts.

This difference in significance means that the repercussions for breaching a warranty are more limited compared to breaching a condition. The most notable limitation is that the innocent party, upon a breach of warranty, does not have the option to terminate the contract.

Instead, the remedies available are typically restricted to seeking damages for the breach. This distinction emphasises the lesser impact of warranties on the overall structure and execution of the contract, primarily focusing on compensation rather than the potential dissolution of the contractual relationship.

Imagine a company, FastTech, purchases a batch of computers from a supplier, CompWorld, for its new office. In their contract, CompWorld warrants that each computer will come with a high-quality graphics card. This warranty is an ancillary term to the contract's primary purpose, which is the supply of computers.

A few weeks after the delivery, FastTech discovered that some computers had a lower-quality graphics card than warranted. While significant, This breach of warranty does not undermine the contract's primary purpose – the provision of computers. As such, FastTech cannot terminate the entire contract over this issue.

However, they are entitled to seek damages from CompWorld for the breach of warranty. The damages would aim to compensate FastTech for the difference in value between the promised high-quality graphics cards and the lower-quality ones provided.

This scenario demonstrates how a breach of warranty, a secondary aspect of a contract, leads to compensation rather than the right to end the contractual agreement.

3.3 Understanding Innominate Terms in Contracts

An innominate term in a contract is a term that is not clearly defined as either a condition or a warranty when the contract is formed. Its classification as either critical or ancillary to the contract is ambiguous, and the severity of the consequences of a breach is uncertain. This ambiguity means that the response to a breach of an innominate term is determined by examining the impact of the breach.

Suppose a breach of an innominate term results in the innocent party losing a substantial part or the entirety of the contract's benefit. In that case, the term will be treated similarly to a condition. In such cases, the innocent party is entitled to terminate the contract. However, if the breach is minor or only tangentially affects the contract's primary purpose, it is considered a warranty breach. Under these circumstances, the innocent party's remedy is limited to claiming damages without the option to dissolve the contract.

The treatment of an innominate term thus depends on the breach's effect on the contract's overall fulfilment, with the court's assessment focusing on the breach's significance concerning the contract's primary objectives.

Consider a scenario where a restaurant, Gourmet Bistro, enters into a contract with a supplier, FreshFoods Ltd., to deliver premium ingredients every week. The contract includes a term that FreshFoods must deliver the ingredients by 7:00 AM each Monday. However, the contract does not specify whether this timing is a condition (essential term) or a warranty (secondary term).

One week, FreshFoods will deliver the ingredients at 9:00 AM instead of the agreed time of 7:00 AM. Gourmet Bistro claims this is a breach of a critical term and seeks to terminate the contract. The court must now decide whether the late delivery term is a condition or a warranty – in other words, whether it's an innominate term.

Suppose the court determines that receiving ingredients by 7:00 AM is crucial for the restaurant's operations (perhaps because it impacts their preparation for lunch service). In that case, the term may be treated as a condition. In this case, Gourmet Bistro could be entitled to terminate the contract due to the breach.

Conversely, if the court finds that the delay had a minimal impact on the restaurant's operations (e.g., the restaurant could still prepare meals on time), then the term may be treated as a warranty. Here, Gourmet Bistro would only be entitled to claim damages for any minor inconveniences caused by the late delivery but not to terminate the entire contract.

This scenario demonstrates how the categorisation and consequent legal implications of an innominate term depend on the significance of the breach in the context of the contract's overall purpose.

3.4 The Concept of 'Time is of the Essence' in Contracts

In contractual agreements, the importance of timely performance is captured by the phrase 'time is of the essence'. This concept determines the rights of the innocent party when the other party fails to perform their obligations within the contractually stipulated time frame.

Whether time is considered 'of the essence' for a particular obligation significantly influences the remedies available during a delay.

(a) **Time as a Condition:** If time is of the essence for a specific obligation, timely performance is crucial and is regarded as a condition of the contract. In such cases, any delay in performance can be treated as a breach of a condition, allowing the innocent party to terminate the contract and seek damages.

(b) **Time as a Warranty:** If time is not of the essence, timely performance is treated more as a warranty. Here, late performance does not provide grounds for contract termination. In this scenario, the innocent party's remedy is limited to claiming damages for the delay.

Many contracts explicitly state whether time is of the essence for certain obligations. In commercial contracts, there is often a general presumption that time is of the essence for delivery obligations if a specific delivery time has been agreed upon. This presumption places a higher importance on adhering to the agreed timelines, with more severe consequences for delays.

Imagine a scenario where a catering company, Delightful Catering, is contracted to provide food and services for an event organised by EventPro Ltd. The contract explicitly states that Delightful Catering must deliver the food and set it up by 1:00 PM on the event day, specifying that "time is of the essence" for this obligation.

On the event day, Delightful Catering experienced unexpected delays and arrived at 2:00 PM, an hour late. Due to the stipulation that time is of the essence for the delivery and setup, this one-hour delay is not just a minor infringement but a breach of a condition of the contract. EventPro Ltd, as the innocent party, is significantly impacted by this delay, disrupting the event schedule.

Given the breach of a condition, EventPro Ltd is entitled to terminate the contract with Delightful Catering. Furthermore, EventPro Ltd can seek damages for any losses incurred due to the late arrival, such as the cost of arranging last-minute alternative catering or compensation for the dissatisfaction of the event attendees.

This example demonstrates the significant implications when time is a crucial element of a contract's obligations, transforming delays from minor issues into potential grounds for contract termination and damages.

4. Inclusion of Express Terms in Contracts

For a term to be validly included in a contract, regardless of whether the contract is oral or written, the parties involved must have reasonable notice of the term. This principle ensures that all express terms - expressly stated and agreed upon by the parties - are recognised and understood by each party when entering the contract.

Reasonable notice implies that the terms must be presented and accessible to all parties, allowing them to comprehend the obligations and rights they are agreeing to.
In written contracts, the contract documentation should clearly outline the terms without being hidden or obscured. Oral contracts require that the terms be explicitly communicated and acknowledged during the contract discussions.

The requirement for reasonable notice is a safeguard against unexpected or undisclosed obligations being imposed on any party. It upholds the principle of informed consent in contractual agreements, ensuring that all parties clearly understand their committing terms.

Imagine a scenario where a customer, Alice, signs up for a gym membership at FitnessPro Gym. The membership contract includes an express term that states members must pay a penalty fee for cancelling their membership before 12 months. This term, however, is written in tiny print at the bottom of the contract and is not discussed verbally at any point during the sign-up process.

Several months later, Alice cancels her membership and is informed about the penalty fee. She contests this, arguing that she was not given reasonable notice of this term.

In this situation, because the penalty fee term was not clearly and prominently communicated to Alice (being in small print and not verbally discussed), it could be argued that Alice did not have reasonable notice of this term when she signed the contract. As a result, a court or tribunal might rule that the term is not enforceable against her. This example underscores the necessity for clear communication and visibility of all express terms to ensure that all parties are fully aware of the contractual obligations they are agreeing to.

The Process of Incorporating Terms into Contracts:

The concept of 'incorporating terms' into a contract relates to how specific terms, such as pricing in the earlier example, become an integral part of the contract. It's common for various terms to be incorporated into an oral contract during negotiations or discussions. Terms can also be included in written contracts, although this can be more complex. The issue of incorporating terms becomes particularly significant when dealing with written exclusions of liability.

4.1 Understanding the Parol Evidence Rule

The parol evidence rule is a legal principle applied in written contracts. It serves as a guideline for determining whether external evidence that is not part of the written contract can be considered to modify, contradict, or add to the terms of that contract. Generally, there is a presumption against using such external evidence, whether in written form (like previous correspondence) or oral, to alter the explicit terms of a written agreement.

However, there are exceptions to this rule. One notable exception is the presence of implied terms, which can be integrated into the contract despite needing to be explicitly stated in the written document. Another exception occurs in cases involving a collateral contract. Here, the courts may recognise the existence of two separate contracts: the primary written contract and a secondary oral collateral contract.

Additionally, the parol evidence rule may not apply if the court determines that the contract was always intended to be partly written and partly oral, with the verbal components being an essential part of the agreement from the outset.

4.2 Significance of the Entire Agreement Clause in Contracts

An entire agreement clause is frequently included in written contracts, stating that the document encompasses the complete agreement between the parties involved.

The primary function of this clause is to reinforce the parol evidence rule. It seeks to prevent the introduction of additional written or oral evidence that could be construed as part of the contract, thereby ensuring that the contract is contained entirely within the written document.

This type of clause plays a crucial role in clarifying the scope of the agreement and limiting the potential for disputes over unrecorded or informal discussions. By explicitly stating that the written contract represents the complete agreement, it aims to provide clarity and certainty to the contractual relationship. The courts generally support the enforcement of all agreement clauses, recognising their value in delineating the boundaries of the contractual terms.

However, an exception arises if such a clause is used as a means for a party to escape liability for misrepresentation. In cases where an entire agreement clause is perceived as a tool to mislead or deceive the other party, the courts may refuse to uphold it.

5. Integrating Implied Terms into Contracts

Though not explicitly stated, implied contract terms are understood to be part of the agreement and are equally binding as express terms. These terms can function as conditions, warranties, or innominate terms and are a significant exception to the parol evidence rule.

Terms may be implied in various **ways**:

(a) **Through Legislation:** Specific statutes may embed certain terms into contracts.

(b) **By Judicial Rulings:** Courts may introduce terms based on principles of fairness or necessity.

(c) **Via Established Practice:** Industry norms or customs can imply specific terms.

(d) **Through Recurring Interactions:** A history of dealings between the parties can establish implicit terms.

5.1 Statutorily Implied Terms

Terms implied by legislation form an integral part of contracts, especially in consumer transactions. Significant sources for such terms are the Sale of Goods Act 1979 (SOGA), the Consumer Rights Act 2015 (CRA), and the Supply of Goods and Services Act 1982 (SGSA). These statutes ensure contracts for goods and services contain essential terms about rightful ownership, suitability for purpose, and quality standards.

While the CRA addresses business-to-consumer relationships, the SOGA and SGSA apply more broadly, including private and business-to-business sales, focusing on goods' quality, description, and ownership.

5.2 Key Aspects of the Sale of Goods Act 1979

(a) **SGA's Implied Terms.** The SGA includes vital implied terms such as the seller's legal right to sell the goods and stipulations that goods must align with their descriptions, be of adequate quality, and be suitable for any purpose specified by the buyer.

(b) **Defining Satisfactory Quality.** As the SGA defines, satisfactory quality covers general usability, freedom from minor defects, safety, and durability, with exceptions for known or apparent defects.

(c) **SGA Terms as Contractual Conditions.** SGA-implied terms are treated as contractual conditions. Breaches permit the buyer to end the contract and refuse payment while returning the goods. Minor breaches are considered warranty breaches, allowing for damage claims but not contract termination.

(d) **Restrictions on Excluding SGA Terms.** The Unfair Contract Terms Act 1977 limits sellers' ability to waive liability for breaches of SGA-implied terms. Excluding title terms is prohibited, and excluding liability for other terms is only valid if deemed reasonable.

5.3 The Role of the Supply of Goods and Services Act 1982 in Contractual Agreements

The Supply of Goods and Services Act 1982 (SGSA) plays a significant role in shaping contracts, particularly those involving hiring goods and providing services. Like the Sale of Goods Act 1979, the SGSA primarily governs business-to-business transactions and private agreements.

For service contracts, the SGSA includes implied terms such as the obligation for the supplier to perform the service within a reasonable time (when no specific time frame is set) and to execute the service with proper care and skill.

These terms introduced by the SGSA are classified as 'innominate terms', meaning that their breach is assessed based on the seriousness of the impact on the contract (as discussed in Section 6.3.3). The breach of such terms does not automatically lead to contract termination; instead, the appropriate remedy is determined by the severity of the breach.

Regarding goods that are part of the service supply, the SGSA imposes conditions similar to those in the SGA, focusing on the quality and suitability of the goods. There is a possibility to opt out of these provisions under the SGSA, but any such exclusion is subject to the constraints of the Unfair Contract Terms Act 1977. This Act requires that any attempt to limit or exclude liability for breach of these implied terms must pass a 'reasonableness' test, ensuring fairness and equity in contractual dealings.

5.4 Overview of the Consumer Rights Act 2015

The Consumer Rights Act 2015 (CRA) is a pivotal piece of legislation that governs the supply of goods and services in consumer transactions, specifically between traders and consumers. It does not apply to transactions solely between businesses or between consumers.

The CRA mirrors some aspects of the Sale of Goods Act (SGA) in that it requires all goods supplied under a consumer contract, including digital content, to be as described, of satisfactory quality, and fit for their intended purpose. The concept of 'fit for purpose' under the CRA aligns with its interpretation in the SGA, and similar exceptions apply.

A notable distinction from the SGA is the robustness of the CRA in terms of liability for breaches of these implied terms. Under the CRA, any attempt to exclude or limit liability for breaching these terms is entirely prohibited, offering more robust protection to consumers.
In addition to goods, the CRA also sets out implied terms for service contracts, ensuring that consumer services adhere to specific standards.

These include:

(a) **Reasonable Care and Skill:** Services should be performed competently and appropriately.

(b) **Adherence to Relied Upon Information:** Services should be carried out in line with any information the consumer has relied upon, such as price quotes.

(c) **Reasonable Pricing:** If no explicit price is agreed upon, the cost of the service should be affordable.

(d) **Timely Completion:** Services should be completed within a reasonable timeframe if no specific schedule is agreed upon.

5.5 The Role of Courts in Implied Terms

While courts typically avoid intervening in the presumed intentions of contracting parties, they do play a role in implying terms into contracts to ensure 'business efficacy' – meaning, they add terms to make the contract operable in a manner that aligns with the parties' apparent intentions and expectations. These are referred to as terms 'implied in fact'. The courts' approach to implying terms is cautious and conscientious.

A term will be implied by the courts only if it satisfies specific criteria:

(a) **Obviousness:** The term should be so evident and self-explanatory to a reasonable person that its inclusion is assumed. This is known as the 'officious bystander test', where it's imagined that if an impartial bystander suggested the term to the parties, they would instantly agree to its obviousness and necessity.

This judicial discretion to imply terms is exercised sparingly and with due regard to the autonomy of the contractual parties. It's a mechanism to fill gaps in the contract that, if addressed, would undermine its practical function and the fair expectations of the parties involved.

Imagine a scenario where a software development company, CodeCrafters, enters into a contract with a client, QuickPay Finance, to develop a custom payment processing application. The contract specifies the features and functionalities of the application but does not explicitly mention the software's compatibility with QuickPay Finance's existing systems.

During the development process, it became apparent that the application was incompatible with QuickPay Finance's current operating system, rendering it unusable for the client. QuickPay Finance argues that it was an implied term of the contract that the application should be compatible with their existing systems.

In this situation, a court might consider whether it was so evident that the application's compatibility with the client's existing system should have been an implicit term of the contract. Applying the 'officious bystander test', if it seems apparent that if a neutral third party had mentioned this compatibility requirement during the contract negotiations, both parties would have unhesitatingly agreed to it, the court might imply this term for the contract to be practically effective (business efficacy).

This example demonstrates how courts can intervene to imply a term in a contract when it is necessary to ensure that it fulfils its intended purpose and aligns with the parties' reasonable expectations.

5.6 Implied Terms Based on Industry Customs

Terms can be implied in a contract based on the customs and practices of a particular industry or market. Suppose there is a widely recognised and established standard within the industry where the contracting parties operate. In that case, it can be sufficient grounds for the courts to imply terms typical for that industry or market in the contract.

However, this practice of suggesting terms based on custom and usage is not absolute. If an express term in the contract conflicts with the industry custom, the express term will prevail. Additionally, a custom will not be incorporated if the contract excludes it.

5.7 Implied Terms from Previous Dealings

Terms can also be implied from the history of dealings between the contracting parties. Suppose the parties have previously engaged in multiple transactions under the same terms (often using standard form contracts), establishing a regular and consistent pattern.

In that case, the courts may imply these customary terms into their current contract. This situation arises when, due to an oversight, the usual terms and conditions are not explicitly included in their latest agreement. The rationale is to uphold the continuity and expectations established through past transactions, ensuring consistency in their contractual relationship.

6. Addressing Incomplete Agreements and Ambiguous Terms

In contract law, courts typically avoid imposing terms into an agreement except to ensure its business efficacy, as previously discussed.

Similarly, when faced with incomplete agreements or vaguely defined terms, courts hesitate to intervene to make the contract viable. If a contract lacks a reasonable level of clarity and certainty, it is unlikely to be enforceable. This is because a lack of clarity often indicates that there wasn't a proper 'meeting of minds' – a mutual understanding and agreement – between the parties, which is fundamental for contract formation.

While the courts aim to respect the parties' autonomy and not interfere unnecessarily, they also recognise the need to enforce agreements that the parties intended to be binding but which may lack complete detail.

Consequently, each case is evaluated individually, with the key criterion being whether the contract, as it stands, possesses enough certainty to be enforceable.

6.1 Instances of Non-Intervention by Courts

Courts refrain from getting involved in agreements where it is not apparent that the parties intend to be legally bound without judicial interpretation or addition. The court will not speculate about what the parties might have intended but not expressly stated. This approach is grounded in the principle that a contract should reflect the actual intentions and agreements of the parties involved. Suppose a contract needs to be more specific or complete for the court to discern these intentions.

In that case, it is unlikely to be recognised as legally binding, leaving the parties without an enforceable agreement. This stance is part of the broader judicial effort to balance non-interference with the practical need to give effect to the intentions of the parties where these can be reasonably ascertained.

(a) **The Concept of 'Agreements to Agree'.** In contractual terms, using phrases such as 'to be agreed' or similar wording, particularly concerning a critical term, typically undermines forming a legally binding contract due to the inherent uncertainty it introduces. These phrases are often characterised as an 'agreement to agree'.

The fundamental issue with an 'agreement to agree' is that it indicates a lack of finality or definiteness in the contract's terms. Suppose a vital aspect of the contract is left open to future negotiation and agreement. In that case, it implies that the parties still need to reach a conclusive understanding of all essential elements of the contract. This lack of a definitive agreement on critical terms means that the contract is incomplete, and therefore, the necessary 'meeting of minds' for a binding contract is absent.

In legal terms, for a contract to be enforceable, all essential terms must be clear and agreed upon. An 'agreement to agree' fails to meet this criterion, leaving a significant aspect of the contract unresolved and open-ended, leading courts to conclude that no binding contract has been formed.

6.2 Judicial Intervention in Contractual Uncertainties

While courts generally exhibit restraint in interfering with contractual agreements, certain circumstances prompt them to actively resolve ambiguities to uphold a contract's validity.

(a) **Addressing Ambiguities.** Courts may endeavour to resolve uncertainties in a contract if they discern a clear intention by the parties to be bound by its terms. Potential situations where a contract may be deemed binding despite uncertainties include:

- **Existence of Resolution Mechanisms:** If the contract consists of a clause allowing unresolved matters to be decided by one party, a third party, or through arbitration. Should these mechanisms fail, however, the contract might be considered non-binding.

- **Familiarity in Commercial Contexts:** In commercial agreements, parties are well-versed in the specific trade and believe they have a binding contract.

- **Long-term Contracts with Flexible Terms:** Contracts intended for future performance over time, where some details are expected to be refined during the contract's execution.

- **Evidence of Partial Performance or Investment:** Cases where one party has already acted on the agreement, either through partial fulfilment or investment, can indicate a binding contract.

(b) **Support from Statutory Provisions.** Statutes like the Sale of Goods Act 1979, the Supply of Goods and Services Act 1982, and the Consumer

Rights Act 2015 can clarify incomplete contracts. These laws may require a 'reasonable price' when no specific price is agreed upon or determinable from the parties' interactions. This provision applies to both goods and services across different types of sales.

(c) **Severance of Ambiguous Terms.** When a term lacks sufficient clarity for enforcement, courts may opt to sever (remove) this uncertain term and enforce the rest of the agreement. The feasibility of this approach depends on whether the removal of the term substantially alters the core agreement between the parties. Generally, the more crucial the term, the less likely the court can sever it without impacting the contract's essence. If severance is unattainable, the entire contract may be void due to uncertainty.

CHAPTER 7. THE LEGAL FRAMEWORK OF EX-CLUSION CLAUSES

Exclusion clauses, as distinct and complex components of contractual agreements, are given a separate focus from general contract terms. An exclusion clause is a provision within a contract that aims to limit or exclude the liability of one of the parties.

The incorporation and enforceability of exclusion clauses are subject to stringent legal regulations, and three critical aspects must be considered:

(a) **Incorporation into the Contract:** The clause must be integral to the contract. The rules concerning incorporating terms, pivotal for all contractual terms, are particularly relevant for exclusion clauses. The process of integrating an exclusion clause into a contract must be unambiguous.

(b) **Effective Drafting for Construal:** The clause must be precisely drafted to ensure it effectively covers the liability it seeks to exclude. This involves clear, unambiguous language that specifically addresses the type of loss or liability intended to be limited or excluded. The precise interpretation (construal) of the clause's wording is crucial to its applicability.

(c) **Statutory Compliance:** The clause must align with statutory requirements. The primary legislation in this context are the Unfair Contract Terms Act 1977 and the Consumer Rights Act 2015. These Acts set forth prohibitions against specific exclusion clauses, particularly those that attempt to limit liability for death or personal injury resulting from negligence. Additionally, they may permit particular exclusions or limitations of liability, provided they satisfy criteria of fairness and reasonableness.

These three considerations form the backbone of the legal treatment of exclusion clauses, ensuring that such clauses are not used unjustly to evade legitimate liabilities and that the rights and protections of the parties, particularly consumers, are upheld.

1. Integrating Exclusion Clauses into a Contract

For an exclusion clause to be legally binding, it must be part of the contract from its inception or before the contract is finalised. This integration can occur in one of three ways:

(a) **through signature,**

(b) **by giving notice,** or

(c) **based on customary practices or previous dealings.**

1.1 Incorporation Through Signature

Signing a contract typically binds a party to all its terms, including any exclusion clauses, irrespective of whether they have read or fully comprehended them.

However, there are **two exceptions to this rule:**

(a) **Misrepresentation Override:** If a party signs a contract due to misleading oral representations that conflict with the written terms, this misrepresentation can invalidate the signed agreement.

(b) **Non-est factum Defense:** This applies if a signatory fundamentally misunderstands the nature of the document they are signing, and what they mark is drastically different from what they thought they were signing. This defence is challenging to prove and is typically successful only when the signatory faces significant comprehension issues regarding the document. Merely not having the document adequately explained does not qualify for this defence.

1.2 Incorporation by Providing Notice

An exclusion clause can also be incorporated if the party relying on it has made reasonable efforts to notify the other party.

The adequacy of these efforts depends on the clause's specific nature:

(a) **Requirement for a Contractual Document:** The clause should be in a document understood as part of the contract. A document issued after the contract's formation, like a receipt, needs to be revised. Conversely, a document, like a train ticket provided at the contract's formation, is usually deemed contractual significance.

(b) **Crucial Timing:** An exclusion clause must be notified before or when entering the contract.

For both methods of incorporation, the crucial factors are the prominence and clarity of the exclusion clause at the contract's formation, ensuring both parties are aware of and agree to the terms they are committing to.

1.3 Incorporation of Terms via Industry Custom and Past Dealings

Incorporation of terms into a contract, including exclusion clauses, can also be achieved through industry customs or established patterns of previous dealings between the parties.

(a) **Industry Custom:** A well-recognised and established practice within a specific industry can lead to the incorporation of a term into a contract. If a particular term, including an exclusion clause, is widely accepted and routinely applied within an industry, it may be deemed to be implicitly included in contracts within that industry.

(b) **History of Previous Dealings:** When parties have a history of engaging in contracts under standard terms and conditions, courts may infer that these terms, including any exclusion clauses, apply to subsequent contracts. For this inference to be made, there must be evidence of a regular and consistent pattern of dealings between the parties. This pattern demonstrates an understanding or expectation that the same terms continue to apply in their business relationship.

The definition of a 'regular and consistent course of dealings' can vary, and courts assess this case-by-case basis. For instance, more than three to four interactions over five years may be needed to establish such a pattern. The courts consider the frequency, nature, and context of past dealings to determine whether it is reasonable to assume that the same terms apply in subsequent agreements.

This approach reflects the legal principle that contractual relationships can evolve and be influenced by ongoing interactions and the norms of the relevant business sector. However, the threshold for establishing this pattern is relatively high, ensuring that terms are only inadvertently imposed with clear evidence of mutual understanding and acceptance.

2. Interpretation of Exclusion Clauses

2.1 Clarity and Precision in Exclusion Clause Wording

Given the potential severity of exclusion clauses in limiting liability, the courts insist that these clauses be drafted with precise and unequivocal language. This requirement is particularly stringent when a clause seeks to exclude liability for negligence.

The exclusion clause must explicitly cover the loss incurred to exclude or limit liability for it effectively. Identifying the nature of the liability is crucial in determining whether the exclusion clause is applicable and enforceable.

Application of the Contra Proferentem Rule:

The 'contra proferentem' rule is a guiding principle in interpreting exclusion clauses. This rule dictates that any ambiguities in an exclusion clause will be construed against the interests of the party seeking to enforce it. If there is any uncertainty or vagueness in the wording of the clause, the interpretation that is least favourable to the party who included the clause in the contract will be adopted.

This rule serves as a legal safeguard against the potential misuse of exclusion clauses. It ensures that such clauses are applied fairly and reasonably, reflecting the intention of both parties at the time of the contract's formation.

3. Overview of the Unfair Contract Terms Act 1977

The Unfair Contract Terms Act 1977 (UCTA) specifically addresses using exclusion clauses in business-to-business contracts. The Act sets out stringent regulations to ensure that such clauses are used fairly and do not unjustly limit liability.

Key provisions of the UCTA include:

(a) **Prohibition on Excluding Liability for Death or Personal Injury:** Any attempt to exclude liability for death or personal injury resulting from negligence is automatically deemed void, irrespective of whether the negligence arises from a breach of contractual duty or a standard law duty of care.

(b) **Restriction on Excluding Other Losses Caused by Negligence**: Clauses seeking to exclude liability for other types of loss due to negligence, such as property damage, are considered void unless reasonable.

(c) **Non-excludable Liability for Title:** Under the Sale of Goods Act 1979 and the Supply of Goods and Services Act 1982, liability for breach of the implied condition of title (the seller's right to sell the goods) cannot be excluded or restricted by contract.

(d) **Limited Exclusion for Description, Quality, or Fitness for Purpose:** Liability for breaching obligations related to the description, quality, or fitness for a specific purpose of goods under the Sale of Goods Act 1979 and the Supply of Goods and Services Act 1982 cannot be excluded or restricted unless such exclusion or restriction is reasonable.

(e) **Standard Form Contracts:** When a party uses its common terms and conditions, it cannot rely on any term that excludes or restricts liability for breach of contract, substantially alters what contractual performance is expected, or entirely negates contractual performance unless such a term is deemed reasonable.

The UCTA thus plays a crucial role in regulating exclusion clauses in commercial contracts, ensuring they are used fairly and reasonably and not to the undue detriment of either party. This regulation is essential in contexts with a significant disparity in bargaining power between the contracting parties.

Imagine a scenario where an office equipment supplier, OfficeTech Ltd., enters into a contract with a small business, CozyCafé, to provide and install a new coffee machine. The contract includes standard terms and conditions set by OfficeTech Ltd., one of which is an exclusion clause stating that OfficeTech Ltd. is not liable for any damages resulting from equipment failure.

Prohibition on Excluding Liability for Death or Personal Injury: Suppose the coffee machine malfunctions due to negligence in installation, causing an injury to a CozyCafé employee. Under the UCTA, OfficeTech Ltd. cannot exclude liability for this injury, as the exclusion of liability for death or personal injury due to negligence is automatically void.

Liability for Property Damage: If the malfunctioning coffee machine also causes damage to CozyCafé's property, OfficeTech Ltd.'s ability to exclude liability for this damage depends on whether the exclusion clause is considered 'reasonable'. The clause is void if deemed unreasonable, and OfficeTech Ltd. may be liable for the damages.

Standard Form Contracts and Reasonableness: Since the exclusion clause is part of OfficeTech Ltd.'s common terms and conditions, its enforceability will be scrutinised under the 'reasonableness' test. If the court finds that excluding liability for equipment failure in a standard supply contract is unreasonable, CozyCafé could claim damages for breach of contract.

This example demonstrates how the UCTA operates to prevent businesses from unfairly excluding liability for negligence, especially in cases involving standard-form contracts, ensuring a balance of fairness in commercial transactions.

3.1 Assessing Reasonableness Under the Unfair Contract Terms Act 1977

The Unfair Contract Terms Act 1977 (UCTA) sets a 'reasonableness test' for specific contractual terms, particularly exclusion clauses. This test evaluates whether including a particular term in the contract was fair and reasonable when the contract was made, considering the circumstances known or reasonably anticipated by the parties.

The assessment of reasonableness involves **several key factors:**

(a) **Relative Bargaining Power:** The court examines the relative strength of each party's bargaining position. A significant imbalance in bargaining power could impact the reasonableness of the term.

(b) **Customer Inducement or Alternatives:** Consideration is given to whether the customer was incentivised to accept the term or if they had the opportunity to enter a similar contract without the contentious term.

(c) **Awareness of the Term:** The court looks at whether the customer was or should have been aware of the term, considering any industry customs, trade practices, or previous dealings between the parties.

(d) **The practicability of Conditions:** If the term involves compliance with certain conditions, the court assesses whether it was reasonable to expect these conditions to be practically met at the time of the contract.

(e) **Customisation of Goods:** Terms related to goods specially made, processed, or adapted for the customer are more likely to be considered reasonable, as they are often unique to that particular transaction.

This reasonableness test ensures that exclusion clauses and similar terms are not used unjustly to exploit differences in bargaining power or to impose unfair conditions on one of the parties. It seeks to balance the legitimate interests of both parties and uphold fairness in contractual relationships.

Imagine a situation where a small business, Blossom Boutique, purchases a point-of-sale (POS) system from a large, well-established tech company, TechGiant. The contract includes an exclusion clause stating that TechGiant is not liable for system failures or data loss. Blossom Boutique agrees to this without fully understanding the implications.

Bargaining Power: TechGiant, a large company, has a stronger bargaining position than the small business Blossom Boutique. This disparity in bargaining power would be a factor in assessing the reasonableness of the exclusion clause.

Customer Inducement or Alternatives: Suppose Blossom Boutique was not offered any incentives to accept the exclusion clause and could choose a similar POS system from another supplier without such a restrictive clause. This scenario would influence the reasonableness assessment, potentially favouring Blossom Boutique.

Awareness of the Term: If it is established that exclusion clauses are not standard in POS system contracts and Blossom Boutique had no prior dealings with TechGiant to know about this clause, the court might find the clause unreasonable due to the lack of awareness on the part of Blossom Boutique.

Practicability of Conditions: If the clause required Blossom Boutique to maintain regular data backups to avoid data loss, and this was a practicable condition, the clause might be more reasonable.

Customisation of Goods: If the POS system was a standard product without any specific adaptations for Blossom Boutique, this might lessen the reasonableness of the exclusion clause.

In this example, the court would weigh these factors to determine whether the exclusion clause in the contract between Blossom Boutique and TechGiant was fair and reasonable. The clause might be rendered unenforceable if deemed unreasonable, potentially allowing Blossom Boutique to claim damages for system failures or data loss.

3.2 Practical Application of Reasonableness in Contractual Clauses

(a) **Limitation Clauses vs. Total Exclusion.** In commercial contracts, it's more common to encounter clauses that limit liability rather than completely exclude it. Such clauses might specify a maximum limit for liability if a party breaches the contract. Courts typically view these limitation clauses as more reasonable than total exclusions of liability. The UCTA explicitly directs courts to consider additional factors like the ability of the party invoking the clause to meet the liability and the feasibility of covering the risk through insurance.

Consider a scenario where a logistics company, LogiTrans, includes a clause in its contract with a retailer, ShopFast, limiting liability for delivery delays to a specific amount. Given LogiTrans's substantial operational size and capacity to insure against such risks, a court will likely view this limitation of liability as reasonable.

(b) **Assessing Clause Reasonableness.** The UCTA assesses the reasonableness of a clause based on the circumstances at the time the contract was formed rather than its applicability to a specific breach that occurred later. The focus is on what the parties understood and anticipated when they agreed.

(c) **Proving Reasonableness.** The onus is on the party who wants to rely on an exclusion or limitation clause to prove its reasonableness.

If a tech company, CyberSolutions, includes a liability cap in its service agreement with a client, and a dispute arises over service quality, CyberSolutions must demonstrate that the cap was a reasonable term at the contract's inception.

(d) **Uncertainty in Enforceability.** Predicting the enforceability of exclusion or limitation clauses can be uncertain. Legal professionals often advise clients on the potential risks associated with the enforceability of these clauses.

A legal advisor might caution a hotel chain about the risks of enforcing a clause limiting liability for damages to guest property. Although the clause might seem reasonable, its enforceability could be contentious, depending on how a court interprets the specifics of a damage incident.

4. The Consumer Rights Act 2015 and its Application

The Consumer Rights Act 2015 (CRA) is a crucial legislation regarding contracts between traders and consumers. It incorporates elements of a European directive focused on unfair contract terms in consumer contracts and explicitly addresses the validity and enforceability of specific contractual terms in these contexts.

4.1 Definition of a 'Trader'

Under the CRA, a **'trader'** is defined as any person operating in a professional or commercial capacity. Specifically, the Act describes a trader as "a person acting for purposes relating to that person's trade, business, craft, or profession, whether acting personally or through another person acting in the trader's name or on the trader's behalf".

This definition encompasses a wide range of commercial activities and is designed to include individuals and entities engaged in any commercial or professional transaction.

4.2 Definition of a 'Consumer'

Conversely, the CRA defines a 'consumer' as "an individual acting for purposes that are wholly or mainly outside the individual's trade, business, craft, or profession".

This definition is intended to capture the activities of individuals when they are not acting in a professional or commercial capacity, essentially when they are buying goods or services for personal non-business use.

The distinction between traders and consumers under the CRA is vital in determining the applicability of the Act's provisions. The Act aims to protect consumers in transactions with an imbalance of power or knowledge, ensuring they are not subjected to unfair or exploitative terms.

However, it's important to note that certain types of contracts, such as apprenticeship and employment contracts, fall outside the scope of the CRA. This exclusion recognises the different dynamics and legal considerations in these types of agreements.

4.3 Terms Prohibited by the Consumer Rights Act 2015

The Consumer Rights Act 2015 (CRA) sets specific limitations on the terms that a trader can include in a contract with a consumer. Notably, the CRA prohibits traders from excluding or limiting liability concerning specific statutory implied terms in consumer transactions.

These include:

(a) **Implied Terms about Goods.** A trader cannot exclude or limit liability related to the implied terms of title, compliance with description, quality, or fitness for purpose for goods sold to consumers.

(b) **Implied Terms about Services.** Similarly, a trader is prohibited from excluding or limiting liability for the statutory implied term that services must be provided with reasonable care and skill. Additionally, liability for breach of the implied term requiring services to be delivered within a good time (when no specific time is agreed) cannot be excluded or limited.

(c) **Liability for Death or Personal Injury.** Any clause attempting to exclude a trader's liability for death or personal injury resulting from their negligence is not binding on the consumer under the CRA, paralleling the provisions of the UCTA.

4.4 Definition of an Unfair Term

Under the CRA, a contractual term is considered unfair if it contradicts the principles of good faith, causing a significant imbalance in the rights and obligations under the contract to the consumer's detriment.

The fairness of a term is assessed by considering the contract's subject matter, other terms within the contract (and related contracts), and the context at the time of agreement.

4.5 Requirement for Transparency and Legibility

The CRA emphasises the need for contract terms to be transparent. This means terms must be written in plain, understandable language and presented legibly. A term failing to meet this standard will likely be deemed unfair.

Additionally, the CRA mandates that any ambiguity in contract terms should be interpreted in favour of the consumer, aligning with the contra proferentem rule applicable to all exclusion clauses.

This requirement ensures that consumers are not disadvantaged by complex or unclear contractual language, fostering fairness and clarity in consumer contracts.

4.6 Consequences of Having an Unfair Term in a Contract

If a term in a consumer contract is deemed unfair under the Consumer Rights Act 2015, that particular term will not be binding on the consumer.

However, this does not invalidate the entire contract. The rest of the contract remains enforceable, and the relationship between the parties continues under the contract's terms, excluding the specific unfair term. The consumer has the discretion to choose whether or not to rely on the unfair term.

4.7 Identifying Potentially Unfair Terms

The CRA provides a list of terms likely to be considered unfair in a consumer contract. This list serves as a guideline and is not exhaustive.

Terms that commonly fall into the category of potentially unfair include those that:

(a) **Limit the trader's liability** in case of a consumer's death or personal injury due to the trader's actions (excluding negligence).

(b) **Impose disproportionately high charges** on the consumer for contract termination or services not provided.

(c) **Allow the trader to terminate a contract** indefinitely without reasonable notice, except in severe circumstances.

(d) **Permit the trader to change the contract terms** unilaterally without a valid, contractually specified reason.

(e) **Grant the trader authority** to set the price after the contract binds the consumer without a pre-agreed price or pricing method.

(f) **Restrict or impede the consumer's right** to legal recourse or other legal remedies.

4.8 Exemptions from the Fairness Test

Specific terms in a contract are exempt from the fairness test under the CRA. These include terms that define the primary subject matter of the contract or relate to the contract's price, as long as they are transparent (clearly expressed and, if written, legible) and prominent (adequately brought to the consumer's attention).

However, terms listed as potentially unfair in the CRA do not benefit from this exemption and are always subject to the fairness test. This provision ensures that critical aspects of the contract, such as its primary purpose and price, can be established unequivocally while safeguarding the consumer against unfair practices in other less central terms.

CHAPTER 8. VITIATING FACTORS AFFECTING CONTRACT VALIDITY

1. Differentiating between Void and Voidable Contracts

This section delves into scenarios where contracts that fulfil standard validity criteria might still be considered void or voidable due to certain undermining factors.

These include:

(a) **Mistake.** Causes a contract to be invalid.

(b) **Duress.** Leads to a voidable contract.

(c) **Undue Influence.** Results in a voidable contract.

(d) **Illegality or Violation of Public Policy.** Renders a contract void.

(e) **Misrepresentation.** Makes a contract voidable.

1.1 The Nature of a Void Contract

A void contract is invalid from its inception and possesses no legal enforceability. An example would be a contract involving an illegal act, such as an agreement to commit fraud. In these cases, the contract is considered null; it offers no legal rights or obligations to either party, and no legal actions can be taken based on its terms. It is as if the contract never existed.

1.2 Understanding Voidable Contracts

Conversely, a voidable contract starts as a valid agreement but may be annulled by the party adversely affected by one of the vitiating factors. It remains in effect until the injured party opts to rescind it.

For instance, if a person is coerced into signing a contract under duress, that person has the right to declare the contract voidable. Until such action is taken, the contract is deemed valid. Rescinding the contract aims to restore the parties to their original positions as if the contract had never been made.

This distinction between void and voidable contracts is essential in determining the rights, obligations, and remedies available to the parties involved when a contract is disputed due to these vitiating factors.

2. The Impact of Mistake on Contract Validity

A contract may be rendered void (not just voidable) due to a mistake, either under common law or in equity. This type of mistake is referred to as an operative mistake.

For a contract to be void because of a mistake, the mistake must be fundamental to the extent that:

(a) **It prevents** the very formation of a contract; essentially, there is no mutual agreement or consensus ad idem, making the contract invalid from the start.

(b) **It results** in the actual agreement being fundamentally different from what the parties intended to agree upon.

2.1 Common or Identical Mistake

A common mistake occurs when both parties agree but are simultaneously mistaken about the same aspect of the contract. Often, this mistake pertains to the existence (rather than the quality) of the contract's subject matter. A contract subject to a common mistake is considered void under common law.

Imagine a scenario where a collector, Alice, agrees to purchase a rare painting from Bob, believing it to be an original work by a famous artist. Bob also believes the painting is authentic.

However, both parties are mistaken – the painting is a replica. This is a common mistake regarding the existence of the subject matter (the original painting). Given that both parties are under the same false impression about a fundamental aspect of the contract (the painting's authenticity), the contract would be considered void under common law.

2.2 Mutual Mistake

A mutual mistake arises when the parties misunderstand different elements of the contract, leading them to be at cross-purposes. In assessing a mutual mistake, courts use the perspective of a reasonable person to determine whether the agreement's terms mean what each party believes. If this test finds that the contract is wholly ambiguous and lacks an explicit mutual agreement, the courts will deem the contract void, as there is effectively no proper meeting of the minds.

The concept of mistake in contract law underscores the importance of clear and mutual understanding in forming a valid contract. When a fundamental mistake occurs,

it challenges the very essence of agreement and consensus, leading to the contract's invalidity.

Consider a case where a language school, Global Languages, contracts with a supplier, TechEquip, to supply 'advanced language modules'. Global Languages believes they
purchase advanced-level language course materials, while
TechEquip understands the contract for high-tech language
software modules.

Since each party has a different understanding of the term
'advanced language modules', they are at cross-purposes. If
a court finds the contract so ambiguous that a reasonable
person could not discern a mutual agreement, it would likely
declare the contract void due to mutual mistake.

2.3 The Concept of Unilateral Mistake

A unilateral mistake in contract law arises when only one
party is mistaken about the contract terms while the other party is, or should be, aware of this mistake. This type
of mistake can void the contract, as it lacks mutual consent or a 'meeting of minds' on the terms.

A typical scenario for a unilateral mistake involves an ob-
vious error, such as a pricing mistake, that the non-mistaken party ought to recognise. The critical factor here is
the awareness, or the reasonable expectation of aware-

ness, of the non-mistaken party about the error. If it's clear that the other party should have realised the mistake, the mistaken belief of one party undermines the formation of a valid agreement.

Imagine a situation where a car dealership mistakenly lists a luxury car for sale at £1,000 instead of its actual price of £100,000. A customer, seeing this, decides to purchase the car at the listed price. In this case, the dealership makes a unilateral mistake about the car's price.

Given the significant discrepancy between the actual value and the listed price, the customer should reasonably be aware that this is a mistake. Since there's no actual agreement on the price, the contract could be considered void due to a unilateral mistake.

It's important to note that, like common mistakes, unilateral mistakes related to the quality of the contract's subject matter generally do not void a contract. The mistake must pertain to a fundamental term or element of the agreement.

2.4 Mistake Regarding Identity in Contracts

Mistakes as to identity arise in situations where one party is under the impression that they are entering into a contract with a specific individual.

In reality, the other party is someone else, often pretending to be the person the first party believes. In such cases, the crucial factor for the courts to consider is the significance of the other party's identity to the contract.

(a) **Identity Not Fundamental.** If the courts determine that the other party's identity was not a decisive factor in the innocent party's decision to enter into the contract, the contract may not be void due to a mistake. Instead, the innocent party might have grounds for a claim based on misrepresentation since they were misled about whom they were dealing with, but the contract itself may still be valid.

(b) **Identity Is Fundamental.** On the other hand, if the identity of the other party was a crucial element in the innocent party's decision to contract – for example, if they intended to contract only because of specific attributes or the reputation associated with that particular individual – then the contract can be voided for mistake. In such cases, the mistake about the identity goes to the root of the contract, undermining its very basis.

Suppose Alice, an art collector, agrees to purchase a painting from someone she believes to be a renowned artist, Mr. X, because of his reputation and skill.

However, the seller is Mr Y, who has impersonated Mr X. If Alice's decision to purchase the painting was primarily based on the belief that she was buying from Mr X. The contract could be void for mistake as to identity. Alice believed she was contracting with a specific individual whose identity was crucial to her decision.

If she had bought the painting regardless of the artist's identity, the situation might have been treated as misrepresentation rather than a void contract due to a mistake.

2.5 The Doctrine of Non Est Factum

Non-est factum is a legal doctrine designed to protect individuals who sign a document under the mistaken belief that it significantly differs in content or purpose from what it is. This doctrine is applicable in particular and limited circumstances due to its potentially far-reaching implications.

To invoke non-est factum successfully, specific stringent criteria must be met:

(a) **Fundamental Difference.** There must be a profound and substantial discrepancy between what the signatory believed they were signing and the actual nature or purpose of the document. This difference should be so significant that it goes beyond details or minor misunderstandings.

(b) **Absence of Carelessness.** The individual claiming the defence must demonstrate that they were not negligent when signing the document. This means they must have had a valid reason for misunderstanding the document's nature.

The scope of non-est factum is narrowly tailored to avoid misuse. The onus on the party invoking this defence is substantial. Typically, success in using this defence is limited to cases where the signatory has particular difficulties, such as language barriers, blindness, or illiteracy, contributing to their misunderstanding of the document.

Consider a scenario where an older adult who cannot read due to poor eyesight is presented with a document by a trusted individual. The older adult believes they are signing a power of attorney document, but it is a contract selling their house.

Suppose the older adult signed the document based on the false representation and could not understand its true nature due to their eyesight.

In that case, they might successfully claim non-est factum to void the contract. This defence recognises that they signed the document under a fundamental misapprehension of its nature, not due to carelessness or negligence.

2.6 The Process of Contract Rectification

Contract rectification comes into play when the parties mutually agree on the terms of a contract. Still, these terms are incorrectly documented in the written contract due to some error. This legal remedy aims to correct discrepancies, aligning the written document with the original, mutually agreed-upon terms.

Critical aspects of contract rectification include:

(a) **Requirement of Common Intention.** For rectification to be granted, there must be clear evidence that the written contract fails to represent the agreed-upon terms accurately. The court will seek proof of the parties' shared understanding or intention regarding the contract's terms.

(b) **Evidence of Parties' Understanding.** The court will examine the evidence to determine each party's actual understanding and intention at the time of the contract's formation. This often involves looking at pre-contractual negotiations and communications.

(c) **Equitable Considerations.** Rectification is subject to fair principles. It may only be granted if it would result in unfairness, mainly if third parties have acquired rights based on the contract in its correct form.

Imagine a scenario where a business, GreenTech, agrees to purchase solar panels from a supplier, SunPower, with a specific efficiency rating. However, the efficiency rating is mistakenly recorded as a lower value in the written contract. Both parties had discussed and agreed upon the higher rating before the contract was formalised.

Discovering the error, GreenTech seeks rectification to amend the written contract to reflect the correct efficiency rating initially agreed upon. Suppose the court finds clear evidence of the common intention for the higher efficiency rating and no third parties are adversely affected. In that case, it may grant rectification to correct the written contract.

Rectification serves as a means to ensure that the written contract truly reflects what was mutually agreed upon, maintaining the integrity and intention of the original agreement.

3. Duress in Contract Law

Duress and undue influence address situations where one party exerts pressure on another, impacting the latter's freedom to enter into a contract. A contract formed under duress is voidable, meaning the coerced party has the option to annul it, but it is not automatically void. The party under duress must actively seek to rescind the contract to invalidate it.

While duress is a common law concept, undue influence falls under equity. Rescission, being an equitable remedy, is subject to equitable defences.

The Requirement of Illegitimate Pressure:

For a claim of duress to be successful, there must be evidence of illegitimate pressure that significantly influenced the decision to enter into the contract. This pressure must be more than just persuasion or influence; it must cross the threshold into coercion.

Duress Involving Physical Threats:

Duress of the person involves physical coercion or threats. To establish this form of compulsion, the coerced party needs to demonstrate that the physical coercion or threats (such as threats to life or bodily harm) were a contributing factor to their decision to enter into the contract. The duress doesn't need to be the sole reason for joining the contract but must be a significant factor.

Jane, a small business owner, is threatened with physical harm by a supplier, BigCorp unless she signs a supply contract with inflated prices. Fearing for her safety, Jane signs the contract. Here, Jane's decision is influenced by physical coercion, and she could have the contract rescinded on these grounds.

Duress Related to Goods:

Duress of goods typically occurs when one party unlawfully withholds another's goods to pressure them into entering a contract. Proving duress in such cases can be more challenging than demonstrating the duress of the person. The coerced party must show that the retention of goods was an illegitimate pressure that influenced their decision to contract.

A contractor, BuildFast, withholds essential construction equipment belonging to their client, HomeRenovate, demanding additional payment not agreed upon in their contract. HomeRenovate, needing the equipment urgently, agrees to pay. In this case, BuildFast's retention of goods under such circumstances could constitute duress of goods.

3.1 Understanding Economic Duress in Contract Law

Economic duress arises when a party uses their superior financial position to illegitimately coerce another party into entering a contract. Unlike physical duress, economic duress requires coercion to significantly influence the aggrieved party's decision.

Simple commercial pressure does not suffice; there must be a coercive impact on the will of the innocent party, invalidating genuine consent.

Evaluating Factors for Economic Duress:

The courts avoid defining a precise set of criteria for what constitutes economic duress, focusing instead on the context of each case.

Key considerations include:

(a) **Practical Choice:** Whether the threat leaves the innocent party with no reasonable alternative but to agree.

(b) **Legality of the Threat:** A threat may be unlawful, like a threatened breach of contract. However, if the threatening party genuinely (but mistakenly) believes their actions are lawful, it might not be decisive.

(c) **Good Faith**: The nature of the threat – whether made in bad faith.

(d) **Contract Reliance and Protest:** Whether the coerced party sought to enforce the contract or protested against the terms.

Economic Duress in Post-Contractual Variations:

Economic duress often emerges during attempts to modify contractual terms, especially regarding consideration, after the contract has been formed. The standard rules on consideration apply; the party requesting a change must offer something additional in return. This further consideration is sometimes a 'practical benefit' the pressured party gains. However, the revised contract or agreement becomes void if the new terms or considerations are obtained under duress.

A construction company, BuildCo, initially agrees to a contract with a client, CityCorp, at a fixed price. Mid-project, BuildCo experiences financial difficulties and demands a significant price increase, threatening to halt the project if CityCorp disagrees. CityCorp, facing tight deadlines and high costs for replacing the contractor, conforms to the new terms. In this scenario, BuildCo's actions could constitute economic duress. CityCorp had limited practical choices and was coerced into agreeing to the new terms under pressure, making the revised contract voidable due to financial duress.

4. The Doctrine of Undue Influence

Undue influence is a legal principle rooted in equity, designed to address and rectify situations where one party's influence over another is misused or exploited.

The doctrine aims to safeguard fairness in contractual relationships, particularly when one party's decision-making ability is compromised due to the influence exerted by another. A contract found to be influenced by undue influence is voidable, allowing the influenced party the option to rescind it.

4.1 Differentiating from Duress

While closely related to duress, undue influence diverges in its focus and application. Whereas duress centres on illegitimate pressure, often involving coercion or threats, undue influence concerns itself more with the subtler aspects of influence and manipulation. The critical question in excessive influence cases is whether the influenced party exercised their judgement and consented freely to the contract.

Undue influence addresses situations where the pressure exerted does not reach the threshold of duress but still significantly impacts the victim's ability to make a free and independent decision. This influence can be more subtle and manipulative, lacking the overt coercion or threat typically associated with duress.

In essence, undue influence seeks to protect parties who, due to the nature of their relationship with the other party, may find themselves agreeing to a contract not entirely of their own volition. It recognises the complexities and nuances of interpersonal dynamics and how these can unduly sway contractual decisions.

Imagine a family member persuades an older adult to sign over property rights. The family member doesn't use overt threats or coercion, but given the elder's trust and dependency, the family member's influence is significant. I

f the elder later contends that the family member's manipulation unduly influenced their decision, the contract could be voidable under the doctrine of undue influence. The court would assess whether the elder honestly acted out of free will or if the family member's influence significantly swayed the decision.

4.2 Requirements for Establishing Undue Influence

Undue influence, as a legal concept, lacks a precise, universally accepted definition but is generally understood through case law as coercion by an external source for personal gain. It can be established in two ways: actual undue and presumed undue influence, leading to the same legal outcome but through different methods.

(a) **Actual Undue Influence.** Actual undue influence involves the influence party's need to demonstrate that they were subject to overt, improper pressure by the other party, leading them to enter the contract. This pressure can be direct, like threats or blackmail, or indirect, such as deceit or exploitation in a trust-based relationship. While similar to duress, the critical distinction lies in the conduct.

Unlike duress, the behaviour under undue influence does not need to be unlawful or in bad faith but rather involves an excessive exertion of influence or abuse of a relationship. The influenced party needs to show that the undue influence contributed to their decision, though not necessarily the sole or primary reason. Once established, the burden shifts and there's no need to prove that the transaction was disadvantageous to them.

A financial advisor, exploiting their influence over an elderly client, pressures them into investing in a high-risk scheme that benefits the advisor. The client, relying on the advisor's expertise, agrees, unaware of the risks involved.

(b) Presumed Undue Influence. Presumed undue influence arises in trust and confidence relationships. This includes fiduciary relationships (like partners in a business or directors of a company) and other relational dynamics (like parent-child, doctor-patient, guardian-ward, or lawyer-client). Trust and confidence must be proven in some relationships, such as between spouses.

Undue influence is presumed when there's a trust-based relationship and the transaction appears inexplicable or suspicious. For instance, a disproportionately large gift in a relationship might raise questions. If undue influence is presumed, the onus is on the influencer to demonstrate that there was no undue influence and that the other party acted freely and with complete understanding. Obtaining independent advice prior to the contract can be strong evidence against undue influence, but it's not definitive.

A therapist recommends the patient invest in a business venture, and the patient agrees, influenced by the trust in their therapeutic relationship. The unusual nature of this transaction could lead to a presumption of undue influence, shifting the burden to the therapist to prove the absence of undue influence.

4.3 Undue Influence Exerted by a Third Party

Undue influence in contractual agreements can also occur through the actions of a third party. This situation arises when someone not a direct party to the contract exerts influence over one of the contracting parties, leading to questions about the agreement's validity.

(a) **Scenario Involving a Third Party.** The concept of third-party undue influence typically involves situations where the influencer, although not a signatory to the contract, has a close relationship with one of the parties and uses this relationship to influence the contract's terms. Common examples include a spouse or an immediate family member exerting influence.

(b) **Obligation of the Other Contracting Party.** When one party to the contract suspects or is aware of potential undue influence by a third party, they have a responsibility to take reasonable measures to ensure that the other party is entering the contract freely and independently. This might include ensuring that the influenced party receives independent legal advice.

(c) **Nature of Third-Party Influence.** The undue influence exerted by the third party can be actual, where specific acts of influence are identifiable or presumed, based on the relationship between the third party and the influenced individual. Supposed undue influence is often invoked in cases where there is an inherent power imbalance in the relationship, such as between a parent and an adult child.

(d) **Consequences of Third-Party Influence.** If a court finds that a contract was entered into under third-party undue influence and the other contracting party did not take adequate steps to verify the voluntariness of the agreement, the contract can be rendered voidable. The influenced party, or the court, may decide to set the contract aside.

Consider a scenario where an older person is persuaded by their adult child to provide a loan to a friend. The friend, aware of the family dynamics, must ensure that the older adult receives independent advice about this transaction.

If the older adult later contests the loan agreement, claiming undue influence by the adult child, the contract with the friend could be voidable due to third-party undue influence. The court would examine the relationship between the older person and their child and the friend's actions (or inactions) in forming the contract.

5. Voidness of Contracts due to Illegality or Contravention of Public Policy

Contracts that involve illegal activities or contravene public policy principles are inherently void and cannot be enforced. These contracts are categorised based on their formation and subsequent execution.

5.1 Contracts Inherently Illegal

Contracts that are illegal from the outset, either due to their direct involvement in criminal activities or because they are detrimental to societal welfare and thus contrary to public policy, are unenforceable. The courts will not recognise such contracts, and parties involved in these illegal agreements cannot seek enforcement or recover losses.

A contract formed to conduct illegal drug trafficking is void from the beginning. Such a contract is unenforceable, and neither party can claim any legal rights or remedies based on it.

5.2 Contracts Rendered Illegal During Execution

There are instances where a contract, legal at its formation, becomes illegal due to how it is carried out. In such scenarios, the party responsible for the unlawful conduct forfeits their legal rights and remedies under the contract.

However, a party not complicit in the illegal act and unaware of the illegality may still have access to legal remedies. If the non-compliant party becomes aware of the unlawful activities, they must discontinue their participation in the contract and cannot accrue any further benefits under it. Courts sometimes have the discretion to remove the illegal elements of a contract, allowing the remaining lawful parts of the contract to be fulfilled.

Consider a contract for exporting goods that becomes illegal when one party decides to evade customs duties through smuggling. The smuggling party cannot enforce the contract or claim legal remedies for any breaches.

If the other party, initially unaware of the smuggling, discovers the illegality, they must cease their participation. They might still be able to seek remedies for parts of the contract that were performed legally before finding the illegal activities.

5.3 Classifications of Illegality in Contractual Agreements

Contracts may be declared void due to their illegal nature, which can stem from various legal and societal norms, including statutory laws, common law principles, moral standards, national interests, and judicial integrity.

(a) **Statutory Illegality.** Contracts that entail actions prohibited by statutory laws are deemed illegal and, therefore, void. These statutes are in place to safeguard public interests and standards, and any contract that violates these laws is unenforceable.

(b) **Common Law Illegality.** Agreements involving the commission of criminal acts or civil wrongs, like torts, are illegal under common law. Sometimes, these may also infringe on specific statutes governing the particular crime or tort, reinforcing their illegal status.

(c) **Moral and Marital Illegality.** Contracts conflicting with prevailing moral standards, particularly sexual morality, are considered void. Notably, societal perceptions of morality are subject to change over time, influencing how such contracts are viewed legally in different eras.

(d) **Governmental Interests.** Contracts that risk governmental functions or national security, such as agreements to trade with enemy nations during war-time, are rendered void to protect national interests.

(e) **Judicial Process Interference.** Agreements intended to obstruct or undermine the legal process are automatically void. This includes contracts aimed at concealing crimes or interfering with the administration of justice.

5.4 The Doctrine of Restraint of Trade

The doctrine of restraint of trade addresses situations where contractual terms limit a party's freedom to engage in trade, business, or employment. Such restrictions are void unless deemed reasonable. This principle balances the protection of one party's business interests with the other party's freedom to work or trade.

Restrictive Covenants in Employment:

Common examples include clauses in employment contracts that prevent former employees from competing with their previous employer or soliciting former clients or colleagues. These are designed to protect the employer's business interests but must not unduly restrict the employee's ability to earn a living.

Non-Compete Clauses in Business Agreements:

Similar principles apply to non-compete clauses in business contracts. They are intended to protect a business's interests but should not unfairly limit another party's commercial freedom.

Determining Reasonableness:

What constitutes a reasonable restriction depends on various **factors**, including:

(a) **Commercial Normalcy:** Whether the parties are in a typical commercial relationship.

(b) **Negotiation and Legal Advice:** Whether the contract terms were negotiated fairly and with the benefit of legal advice.

Legitimate Business Interests:

The courts also assess whether the scope, duration, and activities the clause restricts are proportionate. The party imposing the restriction must demonstrate that it is necessary for protecting their legitimate business interests. Excessive or overly broad restrictions are likely to be deemed unreasonable.

5.5 Voidness of Anti-Competitive Agreements

Agreements that inhibit competition, commonly known as anti-competitive agreements, often fall into the category of void contracts.

These include arrangements where businesses agree to avoid competing with each other, fix prices, or divide markets among themselves. Such agreements typically contravene competition law principles designed to promote fair competition and protect consumer interests.

Critical Aspects of Anti-Competitive Agreements:

(a) **Non-Competition Agreements:** Contracts where businesses agree not to compete in certain areas or markets limit competition and can harm consumer interests, leading to higher prices or reduced choices.

(b) **Price-Fixing Agreements:** Agreements between competitors to set prices at a certain level or within a specific range are inherently anti-competitive. They disrupt market dynamics and prevent fair pricing based on supply and demand.

(c) **Market Division:** Contracts that involve dividing markets or territories among businesses to avoid competition in those areas undermine the principles of free market competition.

While such agreements are critical from a competition law perspective, they are typically addressed in specialised legal contexts beyond the purview of general contract law or the Solicitors Qualifying Examination (SQE). The void nature of these agreements underlines the legal system's commitment to maintaining competitive markets and preventing monopolistic practices.

If two major technology companies agree to avoid selling in each other's primary markets to maintain high prices and avoid competition, this agreement would likely be void as it violates competition law by restricting market competition and harming consumer interests.

CHAPTER 9. MISREP-RESENTATION IN CON-TRACT LAW

1. Criteria for a Misrepresentation Claim

Certain vital elements must be present to establish a claim for misrepresentation in contract law. Misrepresentation involves a false statement of either fact or law made by one party to another, which influences the latter to enter into a contract.

1.1 Directing the Statement to the Innocent Party

For a misrepresentation to be actionable, it's essential that a clear and explicit statement made before the contract was directly communicated to the party who was misled (the innocent party).

This statement can originate either from the party accused of causing the misrepresentation or from a third party. The statement's purpose is to influence the decision of the innocent party regarding the contract.

Imagine a scenario where a real estate agent falsely tells a potential buyer that a house has never had any structural damage, knowing this to be untrue. If the buyer relies on this statement and decides to purchase the house, only to discover significant previous structural issues later, this could constitute misrepresentation.

The false statement about the house's condition, made by the agent to the buyer, influenced the buyer's decision to enter into the purchase contract.

1.2 Key Requirements for Establishing Misrepresentation

To establish a valid misrepresentation claim, certain specific criteria must be met. The misrepresentation must involve a false statement, either of fact or law, that induces another party to enter into a contract.

The intricacies of what is considered a false statement and the contexts in which nondisclosure becomes significant are essential for understanding misrepresentation.

(a) **False Statement:** The misrepresentation must involve a substantially incorrect or legally inaccurate statement. This pertains to current or past facts, which can be verified when the statement is made.

(b) **Distinguishing Opinions from Facts:** An opinion doesn't generally qualify as misrepresentation unless it's not held genuinely or reasonably.

(c) **Promises and Future Statements:** Statements about future events are usually inaccurate for misrepresentation purposes, as their truth can't be determined at the time of the statement.

(d) **Misrepresented Intentions:** A statement about one's intentions can be a misrepresentation if the individual making it knows it's false.

(e) **Role of Silence in Misrepresentation.** Silence or the absence of disclosure generally doesn't constitute misrepresentation. In standard contract law, there's no overarching duty to divulge information, except in relationships involving a deep-seated duty of trust and confidence.

(f) **Contracts Requiring Utmost Good Faith (Uberrimae Fidei).** Specific contracts, notably those requiring utmost good faith, obligate complete disclosure due to information asymmetry between parties.

(g) **The Impact of Partial Nondisclosure.** Statements that are technically accurate but misleading due to incomplete information can amount to actionable misrepresentation.

(h)   **Obligation to Update Information.** If an initially accurate representation becomes false due to subsequent changes, the party responsible for the statement must provide an update. Failure to do so can lead to a claim of misrepresentation.

1.3 Differentiating between Representation and Contractual Term

Determining whether a statement is a representation or an actual contract term is crucial for legal purposes. This differentiation hinges on several principles, including the significance of the statement to the parties, the timing of the statement, and the expertise or knowledge of the party making the statement.

1.4 The Role of Inducement in Misrepresentation

For a misrepresentation to be actionable, the false statement of fact or law must have played a significant role in persuading the innocent party to enter into the contract. The misrepresentation need not be the sole reason for joining the contract, but it must be a substantial factor.

(a)   **Materiality and Reasonableness:** Courts assess whether the misrepresentation was material enough to influence a reasonable person in the claimant's position. The materiality of a representation is gauged by its ability to affect the decision-making process of the innocent party.

If a car dealer falsely claims that a used car has never been in an accident, and the buyer relies on this statement to purchase the car, this could be an actionable misrepresentation, as the statement is material to the buyer's decision.

(b) **Belief in the Statement's Truth:** If the innocent party did not actually believe the misrepresentation to be actual, or if the statement was not effectively communicated to them, or if it did not impact their decision to contract, then it is not considered an actionable misrepresentation.

(c) **Distinguishing 'Mere Puff':** Sometimes, courts may dismiss certain statements as 'mere puff' or exaggerated advertising speak. These are generally not regarded as capable of inducing someone to enter into a contract, as they are often seen as non-factual or hyperbolic claims not intended to be taken literally.

An advertisement claiming that a specific brand of shampoo makes hair "100 times stronger" might be considered mere puffery. A reasonable person would typically not interpret such a statement as a literal fact but rather as an exaggerated claim meant to promote the product.

2. Classification of Misrepresentation in Contract Law

Misrepresentation in contract law is categorised into three main types, each with distinct legal connotations and requirements: fraudulent, negligent, and innocent misrepresentation.

2.1 Fraudulent Misrepresentation

(a) **Origin and Nature:** This type is rooted in the tort of deceit and involves deliberate falsehoods or reckless disregard for the truth.

(b) **Requirements:** The misrepresentation must be made with knowledge of its falsity, reckless indifference to its truthfulness, or without any belief in its accuracy.

(c) **Challenges in Proof:** Proving fraudulent misrepresentation is demanding as it necessitates clear evidence of an intent to deceive or a reckless lack of concern for the truth.

A property owner knowingly omits information about termite infestation when selling a house, falsely asserting the house is pest-free.

2.2 Negligent Misrepresentation

(a) **Statutory Framework:** Governed by the Misrepresentation Act 1967.

(b) **Characteristics:** A statement is considered negligently misrepresented unless the maker can demonstrate they had and maintained reasonable belief in its truth up to the point of contract formation.

(c) **Claimant's Benefit:** The onus to disprove negligence falls on the one who made the statement, making claims of negligent misrepresentation more manageable to substantiate than fraudulent ones.

An investment broker gives advice based on superficial research, inaccurately representing the risk profile of an investment, leading a client to make a loss.

2.3 Innocent Misrepresentation

(a) **Definition:** Represents misstatements made without fraudulent intent or negligence.

(b) **Good Faith Aspect:** The person making the statement should have had credible reasons to believe that their statement was confirmed when it was made.

A vendor of antique jewellery sells a piece, believing it to be from the Victorian era, based on a mistaken but reasonable belief formed from a previous appraisal.

3. Available Remedies for Misrepresentation

When misrepresentation occurs in a contract, the aggrieved party (the innocent party) has access to various legal remedies, the applicability of which may depend on the nature of the misrepresentation.

3.1 The Contract Becomes Voidable

(a) **General Effect:** Regardless of the type of misrepresentation (fraudulent, negligent, or innocent), it renders the contract voidable, not void.

(b) **Options for the Innocent Party:** The party that was misled by the misrepresentation has the discretion to either:

- **Rescinding the Contract:** This means setting the contract aside, effectively returning the parties to their positions before the contract was entered into.

- **Continue with the Contract:** The misled party may choose to uphold the contract but can seek compensation for any losses incurred due to the misrepresentation.

The choice of remedy largely depends on the circumstances of the misrepresentation and the extent of the damages or impact it has had on the innocent party. The primary objective of these remedies is to provide relief and, where possible, restore the parties to their pre-contractual state.

3.2 The Process and Implications of Rescission in Misrepresentation Cases

Rescission is a critical legal remedy for all types of misrepresentation (fraudulent, negligent, or innocent), designed to revert the contract to a state as if the misrepresentation had never occurred.

Rescission effectively nullifies the contract, undoing its effects and returning the parties to their pre-contractual positions. This is distinct from terminating a contract for breach, which only affects future rights under the contract, leaving past accrued rights intact.

As an equitable remedy, rescission is granted at the court's discretion and is not an automatic entitlement like claiming damages.

(a) **Necessity of Notification.** The party desiring rescission must inform the other party of this intention or obtain a court order. Such notification or a court ruling is necessary for the contract to continue. Prompt action is crucial in rescission, and delays might jeopardise the right to rescind.

(b) **The Role of Indemnity.** In rescission cases, the court may order the misrepresenting party to provide indemnity. This financial compensation covers costs or obligations incurred due to the now-nullified contract. While indemnity aids in restoring the original state of affairs, it's a limited form of redress. In many instances, the party affected by misrepresentation might find seeking damages for broader losses more beneficial.

If a company acquires a software system based on misleading information about its functionality, it can opt for rescission upon uncovering the truth. Rescission would invalidate the purchase agreement. Should the court grant rescission, the company might also receive indemnity for installation costs or other related expenses.

However, the company might prefer pursuing damages for comprehensive losses incurred due to the misrepresentation.

3.3 Limitations on the Right to Rescission in Misrepresentation Cases

The right to rescind a contract due to misrepresentation can be forfeited under certain circumstances. Understanding these limitations is crucial, as they determine whether rescission remains a viable remedy for the aggrieved (innocent) party.

(a) **Affirmation of the Contract.** If the innocent party, upon learning of the misrepresentation, chooses to proceed with the contract, this is considered an affirmation. Once the contract is affirmed explicitly or through conduct that implies acceptance (such as continuing to fulfil contractual obligations), rescission is no longer an option. Affirmation is valid only when the party affirming the contract is fully aware of the misrepresentation.

A business discovers that the machinery they purchased was misrepresented in performance but continues to use it for several months before seeking rescission. This continued use affirms the contract, negating the option for rescission.

(b) **Delay in Seeking Rescission (Lapse of Time).** Equity favours prompt action; excessive delay in seeking rescission can nullify this right. For non-fraudulent misrepresentations, the countdown begins when the misrepresentation is discovered or should have been discovered. In cases of fraudulent misrepresentation, the timeline starts upon uncovering the fraud.

(c) **Impossibility of Restitution.** Rescission mandates that parties be returned to their pre-contractual state. If this is impossible due to changes in the
goods' condition or value, rescission may be imprac-
ticable. If substantial restoration is feasible, rescission might still be pursued, although damages might
be a more appropriate remedy.

If a misrepresented antique item is significantly damaged
while in the buyer's possession, restoring the parties to their
initial positions may be impossible, thus barring rescission.

(d) **Rights of Third Parties.** Rescission is not available if it adversely affects the rights of third parties
who have acquired interests in good faith and
without knowledge of the misrepresentation. This
principle protects bona fide third-party rights, especially in cases involving the transfer of goods.

3.4 Damages as a Remedy for Misrepresentation

Damages are a legal remedy available to an innocent
party in cases of misrepresentation. The type of misrepresentation influences the nature and extent of the damages that can be claimed.

(a) **Damages for Fraudulent Misrepresentation.** In the case of fraudulent misrepresentation, damages are based on the tort of deceit. They are intended to restore the innocent party to the position they would have been in if the misrepresentation had not occurred. The scope of recovery includes all losses incurred from the transaction, with no requirement to prove the foreseeability of these losses.

(b) **Damages for Negligent Misrepresentation.** For negligent misrepresentation, established under the Misrepresentation Act 1967, damages are the same as for fraudulent misrepresentation, based on the tort of deceit. Additionally, there may be a cause of action in tort for negligent misstatement.

(c) **Damages for Innocent Misrepresentation.** Generally, damages are not awarded for innocent misrepresentation. However, under the Misrepresentation Act, courts may award damages instead of rescission if it is equitable, particularly in cases where the misrepresentation was minor.

(d) **Damages instead of Rescission.** The court may award damages instead of rescission for negligent or innocent misrepresentation (but not for fraudulent misrepresentation) if it would be equitable. Such damages are not available if the right to rescind has been lost for reasons such as affirmation or lapse of time.

(e) **Measure of Damages.** The measure of damages typically aims to compensate for losses directly resulting from entering into the contract and any related expenditures. This differs from breach of contract damages, which aim to put parties in the position they would have been in had the contract been correctly performed. Damages can still be claimed even after rescinding the contract, and the innocent party is expected to take reasonable steps to mitigate their losses. Any damages received will be reduced by the value of any benefits received from the contract.

4. Exclusion Clauses in the Context of Misrepresentation

Exclusion clauses related to misrepresentation are subject to stringent legal standards, particularly concerning their reasonableness. These clauses attempt to limit or eliminate liability for misrepresentation.

(a) **Reasonableness Standard:** The validity of an exclusion clause for misrepresentation hinges on its reasonableness, which is evaluated under the criteria outlined in the Unfair Contract Terms Act 1977. This assessment involves considering factors like the parties' relative bargaining power, the presence of inducements to agree to the term, and the extent to which the parties were aware or could have been aware of the clause.

(b) **Exclusion of Liability for Fraudulent Misrepresentation:** It is generally considered unreasonable to exclude liability for fraudulent misrepresentation. Given the intentional deceit involved in such cases, courts are highly unlikely to uphold a clause that attempts to absolve a party from liability for knowingly making false representations.

In essence, while exclusion clauses can limit liability for negligent or innocent misrepresentation under certain circumstances, they are less likely to be upheld when it comes to fraudulent misrepresentation due to the inherent dishonesty and potential harm involved.

CHAPTER 10. TERMINATION AND MODIFICATION OF CONTRACT

The concept of "discharge" in contract law refers to the termination or conclusion of a contract. There are various ways through which a contract can be discharged, marking the end of contractual obligations for the involved parties.

(a) **Expiration of Fixed Term:** A contract with a predetermined duration is naturally discharged when this period elapses.

(b) **Specified Event Occurrence:** Contracts may determine that they will end upon the occurrence of a particular event. Once this event happens, the contract is discharged.

(c) **Termination by Notice:** A standard method of discharging a contract is through issuing a notice by one of the parties, as stipulated in the contract's terms.

(d) **Mutual Agreement:** Parties may mutually agree to discharge or modify the contract. This agreement can either end the contract or alter its terms.

(e) **Performance of Obligations:** Fulfilment of the contractual obligations by all parties leads to the contract's discharge.

(f) **Frustration:** A contract is discharged by frustration if it becomes impossible to perform due to unforeseen events outside the parties' control, rendering the contract's obligations unachievable.

(g) **Breach of Contract:** A contract can also be discharged if one party breaches its terms. Depending on the nature of the breach, this can lead to termination of the contract or entitle the non-breaching party to legal remedies.

Each method represents a way in which contractual relations can be concluded, either by the passage of time, mutual consent, completion of the agreed terms, impossibility of performance, or violation of the contract's terms.

1. Discharge of a Contract by Agreement

One of the critical ways a contract can be concluded is through mutual agreement of the parties involved. This method involves either parties agreeing to terminate the contract before its complete execution or modifying its terms.

(a) **Inbuilt Terms for Discharge:** Many contracts include clauses that specify conditions under which they can be discharged before full performance. Typical examples are clauses for discharge in case of a breach or clauses allowing termination upon notice, such as employment contracts.

(b) **Discharge by Mutual Agreement:** Even without specific contract provisions, parties can still mutually agree to discharge a contract. This agreement constitutes a new contract to end or alter the existing one. For this new agreement to be valid, it must meet the standard contractual requirements: mutual consent of all parties and the presence of consideration.

1.1 Situations with Unperformed Obligations

(a) **Consideration in New Agreements:** When all parties to a contract have unfulfilled obligations and agree to a new arrangement to end the contract, the consideration for this new agreement is derived from each party forfeiting their rights and being relieved from their duties under the original contract.

(b) **Binding Nature of the New Agreement:** The relinquishment of rights and obligations by each party under the original contract serves as a valid consideration, agreeing to discharge the contract legally binding.

When a contract is discharged by agreement, especially when all parties have unperformed obligations, the mutual relinquishment of these obligations provides the necessary consideration to validate the new agreement. This process effectively ends the original contractual relationship and obligations.

Suppose Company A contracts with Company B to deliver raw materials monthly for a year. After six months, due to unforeseen market changes, both companies found it financially unfeasible to continue the contract. They mutually agree to terminate the contract.

In this scenario, Company A and Company B have unperformed obligations — Company A is obliged to deliver raw materials for the remaining six months, and Company B is obliged to make payments for these deliveries. By mutually agreeing to terminate the contract, Company A is relieved from its obligation to deliver, and Company B is reduced from its obligation to pay for future deliveries.

The mutual forfeiture of these rights and obligations serves as consideration for the new agreement to end the contract. Thus, this mutual agreement to discharge the contract is binding on both parties, effectively terminating their contractual relationship and obligations under the original agreement.

1.2 Discharge of Contract When One Party Has Fully Performed

When one party has already fulfilled their contractual obligations while the other party still has duties to perform, discharging the contract becomes more complex due to the consideration aspect.

When one party has completed their part of the agreement, any release of the remaining party from their unfulfilled obligations is comparable to forgiving a debt. This situation arises because the party who has performed cannot offer any new consideration for terminating the contract.

To validly discharge the remaining obligations in such a scenario, the agreement must be formalised as a deed, as deeds do not require consideration. Alternatively, the party seeking release from their unperformed obligations must provide some form of new consideration.

Consider a situation where a freelance graphic designer (Party A) has delivered a complete project to a client (Party B) as per their agreement. Party B, however, still needs to make the final payment. Suppose both parties later decide that the contract should be terminated and Party B should be relieved from making the final payment.

In this case, since Party A has already completed its work, it cannot provide additional consideration to validate the termination of the contract. To effectively discharge Party B from the obligation to pay without new consideration, the agreement to terminate the contract and waive the payment would need to be executed as a deed. Suppose they opt not to use a deed. In that case, Party B must provide some new consideration (perhaps a smaller payment or another form of value) to agree to discharge the remaining obligation legally binding.

2. Variation of Contracts

Modifying or varying the terms of an existing contract involves a process similar to discharging a contract. The key elements for a valid contractual variation are mutual agreement among all parties involved and consideration to support the modification.

(a) **Mutual Agreement:** Just as with the discharge of a contract, any variation to the contract terms must be agreed upon by all parties to the contract. This mutual agreement ensures that each party consents to the changes being made.

(b) **Consideration for Variation:** For the variation to be legally binding, it must be supported by consideration. This means that each party should either gain a benefit or suffer a detriment due to the new arrangement. If all parties relinquish some rights under the original contract, this can constitute consideration for the variation.

(c) **Variation by Deed:** If the variation does not involve all parties giving up rights (i.e. if there's a lack of consideration for the variation), then the modification must be formalised as a deed. A deed is legally binding even without consideration.

Imagine a scenario where a construction company (Company A) is contracted by a client (Company B) to complete a building project within a year. Midway through the project, Company B requested additional features to be included, which were not part of the original agreement. Company A agrees but asks for an extension of the deadline and an increase in payment to cover the extra work.

In this case, the variation of the contract involves Company A agreeing to perform additional work (a detriment to Company A and a benefit to Company B) and Company B agreeing to extra payment and an extended timeline (a detriment to Company B and a benefit to Company A). This mutual exchange of detriments and benefits constitutes the necessary consideration for the contract variation to be legally binding. If such mutual consideration weren't present, the variation would need to be formalised as a deed to be enforceable.

2.1 The Doctrine of Waiver in Contract Variation

As an equitable doctrine, Waiver offers an alternative approach to the strict requirement of consideration in contract variation. It involves one party voluntarily relinquishing their rights to enforce certain obligations of the other party under the contract.

(a) **Function of Waiver:** Waiver occurs when a party to a contract explicitly or implicitly indicates that they will not insist on the other party fulfilling a specific contractual obligation. This waiver can be temporary or conditional and does not necessarily require any consideration.

(b) **Limitations of Waiver:** A vital aspect of the waiver doctrine is its revocability. The party who waives their rights retains the ability to revert to the contract's original terms by issuing reasonable notice to the other party. This means that the waiver is not permanent, and the waived obligations can be reinstated.

(c) **Implications:** While waiver provides flexibility in enforcing contract terms, it does not permanently alter the contract. It is more of a temporary or conditional suspension of certain rights or obligations rather than a permanent change or variation in the contract terms.

Suppose a commercial lease agreement tenant faces unexpected financial difficulties and cannot pay rent on time. The landlord may choose to waive the timely payment clause for a few months, allowing the tenant extra time to pay without imposing late fees or seeking eviction.

However, this waiver does not permanently change the rent payment terms of the lease. The landlord can notify the tenant at any time that they will enforce the original terms going forward, requiring timely payments as initially agreed. The waiver here is a temporary suspension of the landlord's right to enforce the convenient payment clause, not a permanent variation of the lease agreement.

2.2 Implied Variation or Waiver in Contracts

In real-world scenarios, contractual relations often evolve through the actions and practices of the parties involved, even without explicit communication. This evolution can lead to what is known as an implied variation or waiver of the contract.

(a) **Implied Variation:** When the parties to a contract act in a manner that suggests a mutual understanding different from the original terms, the courts may infer an implied contract variation. For an implied variation to be legally recognised, there must be evidence of all parties consenting to the new arrangement. Additionally, this variation must be supported by consideration — each party must either gain a benefit or endure a detriment due to the changed terms.

Consider a situation where a software development firm and a client have a contract stipulating monthly updates. Over time, without explicitly discussing it, updates start occurring bi-monthly, and both parties adjust their schedules and expectations accordingly. The courts might view this as an implied variation of the contract, provided there's evidence that both parties have knowingly and consistently adhered to this new schedule.

(b) **Implied Waiver:** If the altered practice or understanding lacks consideration, it may still give rise to an implied waiver. In such cases, a party may be seen as temporarily or conditionally relinquishing their rights to enforce specific contract terms. Unlike variation, waiver does not necessitate consideration and can be more transient or conditional.

In a commercial lease, the agreement might state that rent is due on the first of each month. However, if the landlord consistently accepts rent on the 15th without objection or penalty for several months, this might be interpreted as an implied waiver of the original due date. However, this waiver can be rescinded with reasonable notice, returning to the terms initially agreed upon in the lease.

3. Completion of Contractual Obligations

The process of discharging a contract through fulfilling its obligations, known as performance, typically follows specific legal principles and exceptions.

The foundational rule in contract law is that a contract is discharged only by complete and precise performance. Thus, partial completion of contractual obligations generally does not suffice for terminating the contract.

3.1 Consideration of Substantial Performance

(a) **Legal Adaptability:** Recognising that strict adherence to complete performance can sometimes be inequitable, the law allows for the concept of "substantial performance".

(b) **The essence of Substantial Performance:** This concept implies that fulfilling the core terms of a contract to a significant degree may be acceptable, treating any minor unfulfilled aspects as breaches of warranty rather than as a failure to discharge the contract.

A builder nearly completes a house construction but omits some minor fittings. The homeowner may still be obliged to pay a significant portion of the agreed price, deducting costs for the unfinished work.

3.2 Application to Divisible Contracts

(a) **Characteristics of Divisible Contracts:** These contracts can be segmented into independent parts, each with specific obligations and remunerations.

(b) **Payment Mechanism:** In such contracts, completion of each segment can lead to corresponding payments, contrasting with lump sum contracts that require full completion for any payment.

A supplier agreeing to deliver goods monthly gets paid for each instalment upon delivery, making each instalment a distinct part of the contract.

3.3 Handling Partial Performance

(a) **Acceptance and Contract Variation:** If the other party willingly accepts partial performance, this might lead to an implied variation of the contract terms. Such variation is binding only if supported by consideration, typically established if a new price is negotiated.

(b) **Payment on a Quantum Meruit Basis:** When no revised price is set, remuneration for the partially performed contract is calculated based on the value of the work performed, known as quantum Meruit.

(c) **Conditions of Implied Acceptance**: Accepting partial performance without any choice does not inherently imply agreement to new contract terms.

> If a landscaping contract is terminated before completion, the landscaper might be compensated for the portion of work completed, calculated on a quantum meruit basis.

3.4 Impediments to Performance

(a) **Breach from Prevention of Performance:** If a party actively hinders the other from fulfilling their contractual duties, this could be considered a breach of condition, enabling the hindered party to terminate the contract and seek damages.

(b) **Differentiation from Contract Frustration:** A contract becomes 'frustrated' when it becomes unfeasible to perform, which is distinct from a party being prevented from acting by the other party's actions.

4. Contractual Breach and its Implications

A breach of contract represents a failure to uphold the terms agreed upon in a contract. This failure can manifest in different forms and has varying consequences based on the nature of the breach.

Types of Breach:

(a) **Actual Breach** occurs when a party fails to perform its obligations as stipulated in the contract, either by not performing at all or by performing inadequately or defectively.

(b) **Anticipatory Breach:** Arises when a party explicitly indicates, either through words or actions, that they will not fulfil their future obligations under the contract.

Consequences of Breach: The impact of a breach and the remedies available to the non-breaching (innocent) party depend on the severity and type of the breach.

(a) **Repudiation or Breach of Condition:** If the breach amounts to a total repudiation of the contract or involves the breach of a critical term (condition), the innocent party can either terminate the contract and seek damages or continue (affirm) the contract. The choice to complete must be communicated to the breaching party.

(b) **Breach of Warranty:** If the breach involves a less central term (warranty), the non-breaching party's recourse is limited to seeking damages.

Actions Following Breach:

(a) **Termination of Contract:** The innocent party can consider the contract terminated, thereby relieving themselves from future obligations while retaining the right to claim damages for the breach.

(b) **Affirmation of Contract:** Alternatively, the innocent party may opt to affirm the contract, which means they choose to continue despite the breach. This decision precludes the right to terminate the contract later based on that breach but allows for claims of damages resulting from the breach.

In essence, the response to a contractual breach depends significantly on the type and impact of the breach, providing the innocent party with options to either end the contractual relationship or continue under it while seeking appropriate compensation.

4.1 Differentiating between Termination for Breach and Rescission of a Voidable Contract

The distinction between terminating a contract due to a breach and rescinding a voidable contract is pivotal, as each has distinct legal outcomes and remedial implications.

(a) **Termination for Breach.** Termination for Breach is invoked when one party fails to meet its contractual obligations, effectively ending the contract. Any rights and obligations accrued before this termination still stand despite this termination. The non-breaching party retains the right to claim damages for losses incurred due to the breach.

(b) **Handling Goods Delivered Under the Contract.** Handling Goods Delivered Under the Contract involves specific considerations when the goods delivered do not conform to the contract's terms. The buyer must not pay for these non-conforming goods but must return them. Additionally, the buyer can claim damages for the supplier's failure to deliver goods that meet the contract's specifications.

(c) **Rescission of a Voidable Contract.** Rescission of a Voidable Contract treats the contract as if it had never been effective. This applies to legally valid contracts but is flawed due to factors like misrepresentation or undue influence. The objective is to restore the innocent party to the position they would have been in had the contract not been made, which may include the return of goods or financial compensation.

In essence, while termination for breach addresses the end of a contract due to non-fulfilment of obligations, with accrued obligations remaining enforceable, rescission nullifies a fundamentally flawed contract, aiming to reverse its effects altogether. Each process leads to different legal procedures and outcomes.

4.2 Confirmation after Breach

When a breach occurs, if the non-breaching party proceeds with the contract or behaves in a manner suggesting they accept the contract's continued validity (such as retaining defective goods despite being aware of their faults), this constitutes confirmation of the contract. Post-confirmation, the option to terminate due to that specific breach is lost.

Therefore, if the non-breaching party wishes to retain their right to remove, they must avoid actions that could be interpreted as confirmation of the contract.

4.3 Breach at the Time of Performance

This occurs when a party fails to meet their contractual obligations precisely when those obligations are due, with no prior indication of such failure. In cases where earlier signs of a potential breach are evident, the situation would be categorised as a preemptive breach instead.

4.4 Preemptive Breach

A preemptive breach happens when one party signals explicitly or implicitly that they will not fulfil their contract duties before their obligation performance is due. Suppose this breach involves a fundamental condition or is crucial to the contract. In that case, the non-breaching party gains the immediate right to acknowledge the breach, terminate the contract, and seek damages. They are required to start on the originally scheduled performance date.

However, electing to remain and maintain the contract until the due date is a viable choice, preserving their rights under the contract until that point. Continuing the contract after a breach (confirmation) is a risky decision, as other intervening factors (like the frustration of the contract) could arise, potentially eliminating their rights.

In essence, effectively managing contract breaches demands a careful assessment of the breach type and the non-breaching party's subsequent actions, significantly influencing the available legal remedies and outcomes.

5. Contract Frustration and its Criteria

Contract frustration refers to a situation where a contract is automatically terminated because of unforeseen events that significantly impact the feasibility of its performance. Unlike a breach, frustration occurs without fault from either party and emerges between the contract's formation and its complete execution.

5.1 Criteria for Frustration

Frustration hinges on whether the contract's performance has become impossible or has drastically deviated from what was initially agreed upon.

(a) **Impossibility of Performance.** A contract may be frustrated if its subject matter is no longer available due to destruction or other unavailability, with neither party at fault. This unavailability can relate to essential personnel (due to death or illness) or critical objects. While short-term illness might be treated as a breach, long-term or permanent incapacities often lead to frustration.

(b) **Supervening Illegality.** If a contract becomes illegal to perform due to changes in the law after its formation, this is known as supervening illegality and can lead to frustration. Initially, legal contracts rendered unenforceable by new laws are distinct from contracts that are illegal from the start.

(c) **Radically Altered Performance.** Frustration may also occur when an unexpected event substantially alters the nature of performance, making it vastly different from what was initially agreed upon, even if the performance remains technically possible. For frustration to apply, the alteration must be fundamental and not foreseeable at the contract's inception. It's crucial to differentiate between completely altered performance and situations where partial performance remains feasible.

In essence, contract frustration occurs due to external, unforeseeable events that render a contract either impossible to fulfil, illegal, or fundamentally different in execution from what was initially agreed upon, leading to its automatic termination.

5.2 Factors that do not Lead to Contract Frustration

Not all challenges or changes in circumstances regarding contract performance result in frustration. It's essential to understand what does not constitute frustration:

(a) **Increased Difficulty or Cost.** A contract is not deemed frustrated merely because its fulfilment becomes more burdensome due to increased difficulty or higher costs. The mere increase in expense or complexity in performing contractual obligations does not qualify for frustration.

(b) **Self-Induced Frustration.** Frustration caused by the actions or negligence of one of the parties does not constitute valid contract frustration. In such cases, the situation is typically treated as a breach of contract. The party claiming frustration must demonstrate that it was not a result of their actions.

(c) **Foreseeable Events.** The occurrence of events that the parties could have anticipated at the time of contract formation does not lead to frustration. If one or both parties were aware, or could reasonably have been aware, of the potential for such events, the doctrine of frustration is inapplicable. Instead, the parties might face liability for breach of contract for failing to fulfil their obligations despite the foreseeable circumstances.

In summary, contract frustration is reserved for situations where performance is rendered impossible, illegal, or fundamentally altered due to unforeseen events. However, circumstances like increased costs, self-induced problems, or foreseeable events do not qualify under this doctrine and are handled differently under contract law.

5.3 Effect of Frustration on Contractual Obligations

Frustration leads to the automatic discharge of the contract, freeing both parties from any further obligations. Since frustration is not attributed to any party's fault, no breach of contract occurs, and consequently, no damages for non-performance are recoverable.

However, this discharge can result in financial losses for parties who may have already incurred expenses in preparation for fulfilling the contract.

5.4 Law Reform (Frustrated Contracts) Act 1943 (LRFCA)

(a) **Provisions of the LRFCA.** This statute was introduced to address the potentially harsh consequences of contract frustration. It provides a framework for redistributing losses between the parties. The LRFCA allows for the recovery of sums paid before the contract was frustrated and stopped the obligation to pay further sums. It also permits compensation for expenses incurred before frustration and payment for non-monetary benefits received before the contract was frustrated.

(b) **Exclusions from LRFCA**. Specific contracts are not covered by the LRFCA, including charter parties, insurance contracts, and sale of goods contracts frustrated due to the perishing of goods. Furthermore, the LRFCA's provisions can be superseded by specific terms within the contract itself.

5.5 Use of Force Majeure Clauses in Contracts

Modern contracts often include force majeure clauses to preempt and manage the risk of unforeseen events. These clauses detail conditions under which the contract can be terminated or performance delayed due to events beyond the control of either party, like natural disasters or political upheavals.

By clearly defining these scenarios, force majeure clauses aim to mitigate the need to invoke the doctrine of frustration, providing a predefined route for handling extraordinary circumstances.

In summary, while contract frustration releases parties from their obligations without fault or damages, its impact is moderated by the LRFCA, which offers a fair distribution of incurred losses. Additionally, the inclusion of force majeure clauses in modern contracts allocates risks of unforeseen events, often making applying the frustration doctrine unnecessary.

CHAPTER 11. REMEDIES FOR CONTRACT BREACH: FINANCIAL COMPENSATION

1. Financial Remedies in Contract Breach

Damages in contract law aim to economically restore the injured party to the position they would have been in if the contract had been executed as agreed.

1.1 Varieties of Damages

(a) **Expectation Damages.** This category aims to fulfil the injured party's expected benefits from the contract. It includes costs to remedy any shortcomings or the difference in value between what was delivered and what was promised, as in construction contracts.

(b) **Reliance Damages.** Applicable when it's impractical to determine expectation damages. They cover expenses incurred by the injured party in anticipation or performance of the contract until the breach occurs, essentially resetting the parties to a pre-contractual state.

(c) **Damages for Non-Financial Losses.** These can include compensation for physical injuries directly linked to the breach. Emotional distress damages are generally not recoverable except in contracts centred around personal enjoyment, like vacations. Damages may also be claimed for reputational harm, especially in cases affecting future employment opportunities.

(d) **Absence of Punitive Damages.** Contract law typically excludes punitive damages meant to penalise the party in breach.

(e) **Nominal Damages.** When a breach is proven but no significant loss is documented, nominal or symbolic damages may be awarded, acknowledging the breach without significant financial restitution.

In essence, damages in contract law are designed to compensate for specific losses incurred due to a breach, ensuring fair and just reparation for the non-breaching party.

1.2 Assessment of Damages: Timing and Considerations

(a) **Standard Practice for Timing:** The assessment of damages typically occurs during the contract breach. This point is chosen because it represents when the non-breaching party can start exploring alternative arrangements or solutions.

(b) **Basis for Damage Calculation:** The basis for calculating the non-breaching party's loss is often the cost of these alternative options. In this context, the overarching goal of damages is to financially restore the non-breaching party to the position they would have held if the contract had been fulfilled as per the agreement.

(c) **Situational Variations:** Exceptions to this standard timing can occur under certain conditions. For instance, if the non-breaching party was not immediately aware of the breach or encountered difficulties finding a suitable alternative, the timing for assessing damages might differ.

Imagine a company, ABC Ltd., contracts with XYZ Corp. to deliver specialised machinery by a specific date. XYZ Corp breaches the contract by not paying on time. The assessment of damages would occur on the date the breach (the missed delivery date) was identified. Suppose ABC Ltd. had to rent similar machinery at a higher cost to meet its production deadlines.

The damages would be calculated based on the additional cost incurred by ABC Ltd. for renting the machinery from the breach date until an alternative solution (like delivery of the original machinery or finding another supplier) was in place.

1.3 Remoteness Principle in Contract Damages

Criteria for Recovery of Losses: Losses eligible for compensation following a contract breach are restricted by the principle of remoteness.

For losses to be recoverable, they must:

(a) **Emerge naturally and reasonably** as a direct result of the breach.

(b) **Be identifiable** as probable consequences of the breach, as perceived by both parties when the contract was initially formed.

Determining foreseeable losses is anchored in the context and information available to both parties at the time the contract was entered into, not at the time of the breach.

To summarise, calculating damages in the event of a contract breach hinges on the breach date but may vary under specific circumstances. Additionally, the principle of remoteness acts as a crucial filter in determining which losses are compensable, focusing on those that are a direct outcome of the breach or were foreseeable when the contract was agreed upon. This ensures that compensation aligns somewhat with the expectations and understanding of both parties at the contract's inception.

Continuing with the ABC Ltd. and XYZ Corp. scenario, imagine ABC Ltd. claims loss of profits due to delayed production caused by the late delivery of machinery.

For these losses to be recoverable, they must have been a foreseeable consequence of the breach when the contract was made. If XYZ Corp could reasonably anticipate that a delay in machinery delivery would cause ABC Ltd. a loss in profits, then such damages would not be considered too remote and could be recoverable.

However, if ABC Ltd. claims an unexpected and unprecedented loss, like a decline in market demand unrelated to the delayed machinery delivery, this is likely too remote to be compensated as it was not a foreseeable outcome of the breach of the contract's inception.

1.4 Causation in Contract Breach and Liability for Losses

In contract law, establishing a direct link between the breach and the resulting losses is critical for determining the liability of the breaching party.

The concept of causation plays a pivotal role in this context.

(a) **'Effective Cause' Test:** The primary criterion to establish liability for losses is whether the breach of contract was an 'effective cause' of the loss. This means that the breach must be a significant factor contributing to the loss, though not necessarily the only or primary cause.

(b) **Common Sense Approach:** The courts adopt a pragmatic view when evaluating causation in contract cases. Compared to tort law, the focus on causation is less stringent, with more emphasis on the principle of remoteness in determining recoverable damages.

(c) **Intervening Events:** An intervening event that could have been reasonably anticipated does not disrupt the chain of causation. In such cases, the breaching party remains liable for the losses resulting from the breach.

(d) **Multiple Causes:** The breaching party is still held accountable when the breach is one of several contributing factors to the loss. The court does not delve into distinguishing which cause was most significant.

(e) **Influence of Third-Party Actions:** There are instances where the loss is partly due to an act by a third party. Even in such scenarios, courts may attribute some responsibility to the breaching party and award damages accordingly.

In essence, causation in the context of contract breaches revolves around establishing a logical link between the breach and the incurred losses. While additional contributing factors, including third-party actions or other intervening events, might complicate the situation, the primary focus remains whether the breach substantially contributed to the loss.

1.5 Contributory Negligence in Contract Law

While primarily a concept in tort law, contributory negligence can also play a role in contract law, particularly in cases where contractual duties resemble those in tort law.

Contributory negligence in contracts is considered when there's a breach of a duty that mirrors a tort duty, such as a duty to perform a service with reasonable care and skill, as implied by statutes like the Supply of Goods and Services Act 1982 or the Consumer Rights Act 2015.

The applicability of contributory negligence in contract law has been explored in case law through three distinct scenarios:

(a) **Breach of Strict Contractual Duty:** When the breach involves a strict duty that doesn't require taking care, contributory negligence isn't typically applicable.

(b) **Contractual Obligation to Take Care Without Tort Duty:** If the breach concerns a duty to take care purely within the contract's scope and doesn't align with an independent tort duty, contributory negligence is not a valid defence.

(c) **Concurrent Contract and Tort Duties:** Contributory negligence can be considered when the contractual obligation aligns with an independent tort duty. This is where the defence is most relevant.

It's important to note that contributory negligence, when applicable in contract law, serves as a partial defence. It may reduce the damages the breaching party owes but doesn't entirely absolve them of liability.

In conclusion, while contributory negligence is predominantly a tort concept, it finds limited application in contract law, particularly in cases where contractual duties mirror those in tort law. Its use as a defence is confined to scenarios where both contractual and independent tort duties are present, and even then, it only serves to mitigate rather than negate the liability of the breaching party.

1.6 Calculating Damages for Expectation Interest

In evaluating damages for an expectation of interest in breach of contract cases, the approach to measuring damages varies based on the contract type and the breach's specifics.

(a) **Diminution in Value.** The measure of damages is the difference in value between the contractually promised performance and what was delivered.

A homeowner contracts with a builder to construct a house with specific high-quality materials. However, the builder uses cheaper, lower-quality materials. The damages would be calculated based on the difference in value between the house as it should have been built with the specified materials and the value of the house with the cheaper materials used.

(b) **Cost of Remedying Defects.** This involves calculating the expenses required to correct the breach, such as repairing a product or completing a service to meet the contracted standard.

A car owner takes their vehicle to a garage for a comprehensive service, including engine maintenance. The garage fails to service the engine, leading to mechanical issues properly. The damages would be based on the cost of having another mechanic properly complete the engine service and address any issues caused by the initial substandard service.

(c) **Loss of Amenity Value.** Occasionally, damages are assessed based on the loss of enjoyment or utility, especially relevant in contracts involving personal enjoyment or leisure activities.

A family books a luxury holiday package, including specific amenities like guided tours and gourmet meals. Upon arrival, they find that the tours and meals are significantly below the promised standard, detracting from their overall holiday experience. The damages might be calculated based on the loss of enjoyment and the diminished value of the holiday experience compared to what was contracted.

1.7 Duty to Mitigate Losses in Contract Breaches

In the context of contract breaches, the concept of mitigation plays a crucial role in determining the extent of damages recoverable by the innocent party.

(a) **The essence of Mitigation:** The duty to mitigate requires the party who has suffered a loss due to a contract breach to take reasonable and appropriate actions to minimise their losses. The idea is to avoid any unnecessary or additional damages resulting from the breach.

(b) **Limitation of Recoverable Losses:** An essential aspect of mitigation is that the non-breaching party cannot claim damages for losses that could have been avoided had they taken reasonable steps to mitigate. In other words, losses that result from the non-breaching party's failure to mitigate are generally not recoverable.

(c) **Evaluation on a Case-by-Case Basis:** The assessment of whether the innocent party has adequately mitigated their losses is determined based on the specifics of each case. This involves examining the actions the non-breaching party took following the breach and evaluating whether those actions were reasonable and effective in reducing potential losses.

In practice, the duty to mitigate ensures that while the non-breaching party is entitled to compensation for the breach, they are also responsible for not exacerbating their losses. This duty encourages reliable and proactive behaviour post-breach, ensuring that the compensation sought is fair and justifiable.

1.8 Liquidated Damages and Penalty Clauses in Contracts

In contract law, parties often include specific clauses to predetermine damages for potential breaches. These are liquidated damages and penalty clauses, each with distinct characteristics and legal considerations.

(a) **Liquidated Damages Clauses.** These clauses specify a predetermined sum to be paid as damages in the event of a contract breach. This sum represents a genuine estimation of the potential loss the non-breaching party would incur due to the breach.

Courts generally uphold these clauses if they reflect a true pre-assessment of the loss. The non-breaching party can claim the specified amount without proving the actual extent of the loss in court. Sometimes, these clauses might be contested as penalties, especially if they seem punitive rather than compensatory.

A construction company enters into a contract to build a commercial building within a year. The contract includes a liquidated damages clause stating that for every week the project is delayed beyond the agreed completion date, the company will pay $10,000. This figure is based on a pre-estimated loss the client would incur due to the delayed operation of the building. Since the sum represents a genuine pre-estimate of the losses due to delay, it is enforceable as a liquidated damages clause.

(b) **Penalty Clauses.** Penalty clauses are designed to impose a penalty or a deterrent on the breaching party, often involving a sum disproportionate to the actual damage caused by the breach. Courts are likely to invalidate clauses deemed as penalties. A clause will be considered a penalty if it inflicts a financial detriment that is excessive compared to the obligation breached. To avoid being classified as a penalty, the clause should protect a legitimate business interest, and the stipulated sum should be a reasonable safeguard for that interest. The sum should not be excessive, extravagant, or unconscionable but should instead be proportionate and compensatory.

An employment contract states that if an employee resigns before a year, they must pay $50,000 to the employer. This sum is not based on any estimated loss the employer would suffer due to the resignation but is intended to deter the employee from leaving. The courts would likely view this as a penalty clause because the amount is excessively punitive and not a genuine pre-estimate of any loss the employer would suffer. As a result, this clause would likely be invalidated.

1.9 Indemnities and Guarantees in Contractual Agreements

Indemnities and guarantees are crucial in contracts, providing financial protection and assurance in various situations.

However, their application and legal implications differ based on how they are structured and used in contractual agreements.

(a) **Indemnities.** An indemnity in a contract typically involves one party agreeing to cover the losses of another party resulting from specific circumstances, such as a breach of contract. The scope of an indemnity is determined by its wording. A well-drafted indemnity can allow recovery of losses without the usual limitations imposed by the principles of remoteness, mitigation, or causation. Indemnities can also cover situations where one party agrees to take responsibility for the failure of a third party to perform certain obligations, like paying a debt. This indemnity form is distinct from a guarantee and does not necessarily require a written agreement.

A company, TechCorp, hires a contractor, BuildCo, to construct a new office building. In their contract, TechCorp includes an indemnity clause stating that BuildCo will indemnify TechCorp for any losses or damages resulting from construction defects.

Suppose a construction defect later causes part of the building unusable, leading to financial losses for TechCorp. Under the indemnity clause, BuildCo would be responsible for compensating TechCorp for these losses, potentially bypassing usual limitations like remoteness of damages.

(b) **Guarantees.** A guarantee is an assurance by one party (the guarantor) that a second party (the principal) will fulfil their contractual obligations, such as repaying a loan. Guarantees must be in writing to be legally enforceable. The guarantor's responsibility is secondary and contingent on the principal's failure to meet their contractual duties. The guarantee may become ineffective if the principal's obligations are altered or voided. A guarantor can invoke the same defences available to the principal if there is a change in the principal's obligations.

A small business, ABC Boutique, seeks a loan from a bank but needs more credit history. The owner's parent, Pat, signs a guarantee with the bank, promising to repay the loan if ABC Boutique fails to do so. This guarantee is in writing, making it enforceable. Later, if ABC Boutique encounters financial difficulties and can't repay the loan, the bank can legally require Pat, as the guarantor, to fulfil the repayment obligations.

However, if the loan terms are significantly changed without Pat's consent, the guarantee may become void, and Pat might not be held liable for the loan repayment.

2. Debt Claims in Contractual Agreement

Debt claims in contract law involve the focus on recovering a specific sum owed under the contract terms rather than seeking compensation for losses resulting from a breach. This type of claim is distinct from a claim for damages in several vital aspects.

A debt claim arises when one party seeks to recover a predetermined amount due under the contract. For instance, if a contract stipulates that a payment is to be made for goods or services and the payment is not made, the party owed the money can make a debt claim for the exact amount due.

Key Differences from Damage Claims:

(a) **No Consideration of Remoteness or Causation:** In a debt claim, the focus is on the amount due as per the contract terms, without the need to establish how the breach caused specific losses. The legal principles of remoteness and causation, which are crucial in determining compensatory damages, do not apply to debt claims.

(b) **No Duty to Mitigate:** Unlike in damage claims, where the claimant must take reasonable steps to minimise losses, there is no obligation in debt claims. The claimant is entitled to the total amount owed regardless of any mitigating factors.

The amount claimed in a debt claim is 'liquidated', meaning it is a fixed or determinate sum as stipulated in the contract. Courts typically do not modify this amount unless exceptional circumstances or contractual provisions dictate otherwise.

In essence, debt claims provide a straightforward mechanism for recovering amounts contractually due without the complexities often associated with proving and calculating damages in breach of contract cases. This direct approach is beneficial in commercial transactions where clear payment terms are outlined in the contract.

3. Equitable Remedies Overview

Equitable remedies, distinct from monetary damages, offer an alternative form of redress to the aggrieved party in a contract. These remedies are not automatically granted but are instead issued at the court's discretion, often when monetary compensation is insufficient.

Equity supplements the rigidities of common law, providing remedies where financial compensation falls short in addressing the harm caused.

3.1 Specific Performance Explained

Specific performance involves a court order directing the party who breached the contract to fulfil their contractual duties. This remedy is particularly relevant when financial damages don't adequately compensate for the breach, such as in unique situations like land sales.

However, specific performance has limitations and is not granted in scenarios like employment contracts, where compelling personal service would be inappropriate or where it would cause undue hardship to the breaching party.

3.2 Injunctions and Rescission in Contract Law

In contrast to specific performance, an injunction is a court order preventing a party from breaching the contract, typically applied to negative obligations (promises not to do something). While rare, mandatory injunctions can compel a party to take specific actions. In employment contexts, injunctions can prevent breaches of contract but cannot force an employee to work.

Rescission effectively nullifies a voidable contract, resetting the parties' positions as if the contract had never existed. It's applicable in situations such as misrepresentation or mistake occurring at or before the contract formation.

3.3 Defending against Equitable Remedies

In equity, remedies are subject to fairness considerations, and certain defences can preclude their issuance. These include the claimant's unethical behaviour, the waiver of rights by the claimant, or significant delays in seeking remedy, embodying the principle that equity favours the diligent and not those who delay.

4. Restitutionary Remedies Explained and Necessary Requirements

Restitutionary remedies function independently from contract law, primarily addressing unjust enrichment. This legal concept comes into play when one party unjustly benefits at the expense of another, often due to circumstances like mistake, duress, or undue influence.

Unlike contractual damages, restitution aims to rectify situations where one party wrongfully gains rather than compensates for a loss.

(a) **Application of Restitution:** Restitution becomes relevant, particularly when a contract is invalidated or set aside. In such cases, any benefits gained under the now void contract are deemed to have been acquired without proper consideration, warranting their return.

(b) **Conditions for Restitution:** Restitutionary remedies are typically reserved for exceptional circumstances where traditional remedies like damages or specific performance are deemed insufficient.

(c) **Objective of Restitution:** The primary goal of restitution is to prevent wrongdoers from profiting from their improper actions. It seeks to restore the balance by obliging the party who has unjustly gained to return those gains.

Requirements for Restitutionary Remedies:

Restitutionary remedies focus on repaying benefits that one party has unjustly gained at the expense of another. To obtain restitution, the claimant, typically the innocent party, needs to establish **several key elements**:

(a) **Enrichment or Benefit:** The first requirement is demonstrating that the other party received a benefit or enrichment. This could be in various forms, such as money, goods, or services.

(b) **Enrichment at the Claimant's Expense:** It must be shown that the enrichment of the other party occurred directly at the claimant's expense. This means the benefit one party gains correlates with a loss or disadvantage to the other.

(c) **Unjust Nature of the Enrichment:** The claimant must prove that the enrichment is unjust. This involves showing that the enrichment lacks a legal or contractual basis or occurred due to improper conduct like mistake, duress, or undue influence.

(d) **Availability of Defences:** The court will also consider if there are any valid defences available to the party who received the benefit. Defences might include arguments that the benefit was legally or contractually justified or that returning the benefit would be unjust under the circumstances.

The overarching principle in restitution is to prevent unjust enrichment and ensure that no party benefits unfairly at the expense of another. The aim is to restore the parties to the position they would have been in had the unjust enrichment not occurred.

4.1 Instances of Unjust Enrichment

Unjust enrichment claims arise in various scenarios where one party unfairly benefits at the expense of another without a legal basis.

Some everyday situations where restitution for unjust enrichment might be appropriate include:

(a) **Provision of Work, Services, or Goods Without a Contract** occurs when one party provides work, services, or goods without a formal contract. However, if the underlying contract is void due to illegal severe conduct, restitution may not be available.

(b) **Total Failure of Consideration:** For instance, if a contract is terminated before a party has begun fulfilling their contractual obligations, this might result in a claim for restitution due to the total failure of consideration.

(c) **Partial Contract Performance Accepted Voluntarily:** If a contract is not entirely performed, and the innocent party accepts partial performance without an agreed price, leading to a lack of new consideration, restitution may be claimed for the benefit received.

(d) **Payments Made by Mistake:** When a party mistakenly transfers money to another, a restitution claim can be made to recover these funds.

(e) **Following Contract Rescission with Outstanding Sums:** If a contract is rescinded and there's an outstanding sum of money or property in possession of the wrong party, a restitution claim can help recover it.

(f) **Transfers Under Threat or Pressure:** Any property transfer or money made under duress or undue pressure can lead to a restitution claim to reverse the transfer.

(g) **Abuse of Trust or Confidence:** When a party exploits a relationship of trust and confidence to influence another party to transfer property, restitution

may be sought to correct the imbalance created by
this undue influence.

These examples illustrate the breadth of situations where
unjust enrichment can occur, highlighting the role of
restitution in restoring fairness and balance in such circumstances.

4.2 Forms of Restitutionary Remedies

Restitutionary remedies aim to rectify unjust enrichment,
with the court determining the appropriate form based
on the nature of the enrichment. These remedies can
either return money or property or compensate for services or goods provided.

(a) **Monetary or Property Return:** In cases where
unjust enrichment involves specific property or
money, the remedy often consists of the return of
that property or money to the party who suffered the
loss.

(b) **Quantum Meruit for Services:** When services
have been rendered without a formal contract or a
contract has been rescinded, the court may order
payment on a quantum Meruit basis. This means
the party who provided the services is entitled to receive a reasonable sum for their work, even though
there was no agreed contractual rate.

A freelance graphic designer works for a client without a formal contract. After delivering the designs, the client refused to pay, claiming there was no agreed rate. The designer can seek a quantum meruit remedy, where the court would determine a reasonable fee for the services rendered, ensuring the designer is compensated for their work despite the absence of a formal payment agreement.

(c) **Quantum Valebat for Goods:** Similarly, for goods supplied where no price was set or where a contract was not fully executed, the remedy of quantum valebat applies. This requires the recipient of the goods to pay a reasonable value for them, reflecting what the goods were worth.

A bakery supplies bread to a local restaurant daily, based on a verbal understanding without a fixed price. If the restaurant suddenly stops paying, arguing the lack of a contractual price, the bakery can claim quantum value. Here, the restaurant would be ordered to pay a reasonable price for the bread supplied, based on the market value or usual selling price of similar goods.

4.3 Account of Profits

In rare and exceptional circumstances, the court may go beyond the typical restitutionary remedies and order an account of profits. This is considered when traditional damages are insufficient or inappropriate. Under this remedy, the party who unjustly enriched themselves at the expense of another must hand over the profits made from their actions.

This approach ensures that the party who gained unjustly does not retain their ill-gotten gains and that the innocent party is compensated to the extent of the wrongdoer's benefit, not just their loss. This remedy is particularly relevant in cases involving a breach of trust or misuse of property, where the profits arising from the breach can be quantified.

A company unlawfully uses patented technology belonging to another company in its product, earning significant profits. Upon discovering this infringement, the patent owner can seek an account of profits as a remedy. The infringing company would then be required to hand over the profits earned from the sale of products using the patented technology.

This remedy ensures that the infringing party does not benefit from its wrongful use of the patent and compensates the patent owner for the misuse of their intellectual property.

CONCLUSION

As you approach the end of this comprehensive guide on Contract Law for your SQE1 exam preparation, it's important to reflect on the journey you've undertaken and the knowledge you've acquired. This guide has endeavored to equip you with a deep and practical understanding of Contract Law, a fundamental pillar of the legal system in England and Wales.

Good luck with your SQE1 exam. May your hard work and dedication pave the way to a successful and fulfilling career in law. Remember, this guide is just the beginning of your journey as a legal professional. Embrace the challenges and opportunities that lie ahead with confidence and a commitment to excellence.

REFERENCES

McKendrick, E. (2015). Contract Law. Palgrave.

Merkin, R., Saintier, S. (2023). Poole' s Textbook on Contract Law. Oxford University Press.

Furmston, M. P., Cheshire, G. C., & Fifoot, C. H. S. (2013). Cheshire, Fifoot, and Furmston's Law of Contract. Oxford University Press.

Beatson, J., Burrows, A., & Cartwright, J. (2020). Anson's Law of Contract. Oxford University Press.

Collins, H. (2008). The Law of Contract. Cambridge University Press.

Stone, R. & Devenney, J. (2022). The Modern Law of Contract. Routledge.

Peel, E. (2020). Treitel on the Law of Contract. Sweet & Maxwell.

ABOUT AUTHORS

Anastasia & Andrew Vialichka have authored a revered collection of study guides and quizzes (metexam.co.uk), addressing the full spectrum of topics tested by the Solicitors Qualifying Examination (SQE). Their portfolio encompasses thorough treatments of *Business Law and Practice, Dispute Resolution, Contract, Tort, Legal System of England and Wales, Constitutional and Administrative Law and EU Law, Legal Services, Property Law and Practice, Wills and the Administration of Estates, Solicitors Accounts, Land Law, Trusts, Criminal Law and Practice, as well as Equity.*

Authors' works are not only informational but also innovative, incorporating AI-based technology to enhance test preparation. This modern approach tailors learning to individual styles, aiding students to master both the theory and practice required for the SQE.

www.ingramcontent.com/pod-product-compliance
Lightning Source LLC
Chambersburg PA
CBHW061244220326
41599CB00028B/5527